LINCOLN
FOR BEGINNERS®

WRITTEN BY
PAUL BUHLE

COMICS AND ILLUSTRATIONS BY
SHARON RUDAHL

FOREWORD BY
ERIC FONER

FOR BEGINNERS®

Published by For Beginners LLC
155 Main Street, Suite 211
Danbury, CT 06810 USA
www.forbeginnersbooks.com

Text: ©2015 Paul Buhle
Comics and Illustrations: ©2015 Sharon Rudahl

Design and composition by Tim E. Ogline / Ogline Design.

A For Beginners˚ Documentary Comic Book

Cataloging-in-Publication information is available from the Library of Congress.

ISBN # 978-1-934389-85-0 Trade

Manufactured in the United States of America

For Beginners˚ and Beginners Documentary Comic Books˚
are published by For Beginners LLC.

First Edition

10 9 8 7 6 5 4 3 2 1

CONTENTS

ABRAHAM LINCOLN

SIXTEENTH PRESIDENT

"As I would not be a slave, so I would not be a master"

FOREWORD

Abraham Lincoln is the most iconic figure in American history. He exerts a unique hold on our historical imagination, as an embodiment of core American ideals and myths—the self-made man, the frontier hero, the liberator of the slaves. Thousands of works have been written about Lincoln, and almost any Lincoln one desires can be found somewhere in the literature. Lincoln has been portrayed as a shrewd political operator driven by ambition, a moralist for whom emancipation was the logical conclusion of a lifetime hatred of slavery, and a racist who actually defended and tried to protect slavery. Politicians from conservatives to communists, civil rights activists to segregationists, and members of every Protestant denomination as well as non-believers, have claimed him as their own.

Lincoln For Beginners is a worthy addition to the vast Lincoln literature. In a combination of lucid prose and appealing graphic art, it tells the story of Lincoln's life in a wholly accessible manner, but one deeply rooted in current historical thinking about the man and his times. Both the private and public Lincoln's are ably discussed, as is the centrality of the slavery issue to Lincoln's career and of emancipation to the course of the Civil War. The book makes clear that Lincoln hated slavery from his earliest days, but that his views evolved over time as to how to deal with the institution within a constitutional system that erected strong protections for the system. Lincoln's ideas about the role of blacks in American life also changed—from his early embrace of the idea of "colonizing" former slaves outside the United States, to support at the end of his life for recognizing all African-Americans as citizens and giving educated blacks and those who had served in the Union army the right to vote. That a man with Lincoln's humble origins could rise to the presidency is a testament to the opportunities enjoyed by many Americans, then and now. But the failure of the nation to establish civil and political equality for blacks on a permanent basis after the Civil War left to future generations the difficult task of fulfilling the promise of the "new birth of freedom" Lincoln did so much to bring about.

—Eric Foner

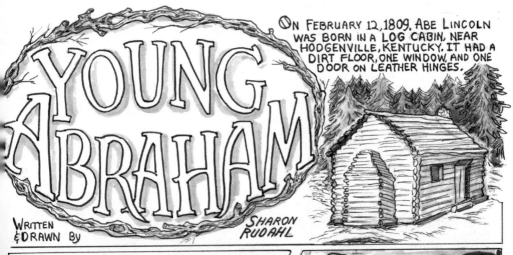

YOUNG ABRAHAM

WRITTEN & DRAWN BY *SHARON RUDAHL*

ON FEBRUARY 12, 1809, ABE LINCOLN WAS BORN IN A LOG CABIN, NEAR HODGENVILLE, KENTUCKY. IT HAD A DIRT FLOOR, ONE WINDOW, AND ONE DOOR ON LEATHER HINGES.

LINCOLN'S GRANDFATHER HAD FOLLOWED DANIEL BOONE THRU THE CUMBERLAND GAP INTO THE WILDERNESS. HIS FAMILY LED THE HARSH LIFE OF PIONEERS SCRATCHING FARMS FROM ANCIENT FORESTS.

THERE WERE FEW COMFORTS — BUT THE LAND WAS RICH AND THE WOODS FULL OF GAME.

WHEN ABE'S FATHER **TOM** COURTED HIS MOTHER NANCY, HE BOUGHT YARDS OF **LINEN, SILK** AND CASHMERE, BUTTONS, THREAD, FORKS AND SPOONS.

THEIR WEDDING FEAST INCLUDED BEAR MEAT, WILD TURKEY AND DUCKS, VENISON, A WHOLE SHEEP, COFFEE AND WHISKEY, MAPLE SUGAR AND PEACH SYRUP.

ABE'S FATHER TOM WAS A FARMER AND CARPENTER WHO ONCE SERVED AS A COMMUNITY CONSTABLE. WHEN ABE WAS 3, TOM MOVED THE FAMILY TO A 30 ACRE FARM CALLED KNOB CREEK CLOSE TO THE DIRT ROAD CONNECTING LOUISVILLE AND NASHVILLE. THIS WAS THE FIRST HOME ABE REMEMBERED.

ALONG THIS ROAD, LITTLE BOY ABRAHAM MET PASSING SOLDIERS, SLAVES, PEDDLERS, MEDICINE MEN, EVEN POLITICIANS, TRAVELING TO THE STATE LEGISLATURE IN LEXINGTON

ABE WAS PUT TO WORK AS SOON AS HE COULD STAND: PLANTING, WEEDING, FEEDING LIVESTOCK, CLEANING ASHES OUT OF THE FIREPLACE, CARRYING WATER, PICKING BERRIES.

ABE'S PARENTS NEVER LEARNED TO READ OR WRITE. WHEN FARM CHORES ALLOWED, HE AND HIS OLDER SISTER SARAH HIKED TO A ONE-ROOM SCHOOL. BUT HE GOT LESS THAN A FULL YEAR'S SCHOOLING IN ALL.

ABE'S PARENTS BELIEVED SLAVERY WAS WRONG. TOM ALSO FEARED SLAVE LABOR WOULD DRIVE DOWN FREE WORKER'S WAGES.

WHEN ABE WAS 7, HIS FATHER WAS SUED FOR TRESPASS ON HIS OWN HOMESTEAD. THE FAMILY MOVED TO WILDER COUNTRY IN INDIANA. SLAVERY WAS OUTLAWED IN INDIANA, AND FARMERS COULD BUY LAND DIRECTLY FROM THE GOVERNMENT FOR $1.25 AN ACRE.

THE FIRST WINTER, THEY SLEPT IN A 3-SIDED SHELTER WARMED ONLY BY A CAMPFIRE.

BY SPRING, THE LINCOLNS BUILT A STURDY CABIN WITH A STONE FIREPLACE AND A LOFT BED FOR ABE.

ABE GREW QUICKLY, TALLER AND STRONGER THAN OTHER BOYS HIS AGE.

"THOUGH VERY YOUNG, I WAS LARGE FOR MY AGE AND HAD AN AXE PUT INTO MY HANDS AT ONCE."

IN 1818, WHEN ABE WAS 9, HIS MOTHER AND HER PARENTS DIED OF THE MYSTERIOUS "MILK SICKNESS." IT WAS CAUSED BY A TOXIC WEED COWS ATE ON THE PRAIRIE.

"...BE GOOD TO YOUR FATHER... ...AND TO EACH OTHER...AND TO THE WORLD..."

YOUNG ABRAHAM WHITTLED THE PEGS THAT HELD TOGETHER THE BOARDS HIS FATHER SAWED TO MAKE NANCY LINCOLN'S COFFIN.

ABE BORROWED BOOKS: ROBINSON CRUSOE, A BIOGRAPHY OF GEORGE WASHINGTON, AESOP'S FABLES...

NEIGHBORS OFTEN SAW HIM WORKING WITH A BOOK IN ONE HAND.

ABE'S OLDER COUSIN DENNIS HANKS SCOFFED AT SO MUCH READING.

"ABE, THEM YARNS IS ALL LIES!!"

"MIGHTY DARN GOOD LIES, DENNY..."

HE AND DENNIS FOUND TIME TO SWOP STORIES WITH OTHER BOYS AT THE GENERAL STORE IN GENTRYVILLE, 1½ MILES FROM THE LINCOLN CABIN.

ABE'S FUNNY YARNS AND SKILL AT WRESTLIN' WON OVER THE LOCAL TOUGHS.

ABE WROTE LETTERS FOR LOCAL FARMERS, USING A CROW QUILL PEN AND INK PRESSED FROM BLUEBERRIES...

WHILE STILL IN HIS TEENS, ABE GREW TO THE IMPRESSIVE HEIGHT OF 6 FEET 4 INCHES. HE WAS WIDELY KNOWN AS CAPABLE AND TRUSTWORTHY

At the age of nineteen, young Abraham Lincoln was hired to help pilot a flatboat carrying corn, oats, beans and meat down the Mississippi River to New Orleans...

On his first trip away from the frontier, Abe saw many wonders: painted steamboats, plantation mansions, crowded noisy cities, ladies of fashion, gamblers and rich gentlemen~ and vast pens where human beings waited to be auctioned off like cattle.

CHAPTER ONE

YOUNG LINCOLN
AND HIS WORLD

There is no greater symbol of the American presidency than Abraham Lincoln—not Franklin D. Roosevelt, not even George Washington. But Lincoln himself, his personality, the sources of his dedication, and his idealism, all remain very much a mystery. The apparently sudden rise to world stature of a hard-traveling lawyer from the frontier, with no prominent family or social connections to back him, was a wonder of the age. Well over a thousand books about Lincoln have been written to date, and still the enigma remains, perhaps because it is also the enigma of a young country finding its footing and its destiny. He surely told more jokes and humorous anecdotes than anyone else in the history of the office, but it is also probably true that no president was more inclined to such deep melancholy. No part of the Lincoln enigma is more profound or more perplexing than his beliefs about god and destiny. Did he invent his own version of religion, as many around him suggested? Why did he avoid going to church for so long, and apparently invent a personal religion, when fervently religious people and institutions surrounded him from his earliest days? How did the horrific death and destruction in the years of the Civil War bring him to biblical judgments?

How did he become to the nation—but especially to African Americans—"Father Abraham," an Old Testament hero with the destiny of millions in his oversized hands?

Lincoln's most widely read biographer, the poet and folksinger Carl Sandburg, described the future leader as too "homely" and homespun, too full of dry humor and physically gawky to be romantic with women or to impress sophisticated society. If many of Lincoln's stories were easy to see through—a way to hide his real feelings as much to offer insight on some subject—his facial expressions, looked at closely, seemed to show something else. Lincoln's "face settled into granitic calm and there came into the depths of his eyes the shadows of a burning he had been through," Sandburg wrote, capturing the impression of many who met Lincoln for the first time and kept the memory close for the rest of their lives. There was a complexity to Lincoln, but only outright political enemies could call him insincere.

David Ross Locke, whose humor columns in the press the president regularly read to visitors at the White House, wrote that Lincoln's sense of humor spared him from overwhelming despair. The wartime burden of becoming the "world's hero" was too much even for Lincoln's strong character, Locke wrote, and in death the fallen leader had "the look of a worn man suddenly relieved."

Lincoln entered regional American folklore as a somewhat strange and remarkable creature even before he became president. In the end, cut down by an assassin after leading the Union to victory and preserving the nation, he became larger than life. Even today, his face stares out from the famed statue at the Lincoln Memorial in Washington, D.C., as well as from prints, photographs, paintings and comic art pieces of all kinds, not to mention the Lincoln penny. He belongs to all of us and to the world ... But who was he?

THE REGIONAL MAN

The great American novelist Mark Twain commented, late in his own life, that Abraham Lincoln's birth in Kentucky made him the candidate to save the United States from a fatal division. "No wintry New England Brahmin could have done it, or any torrid cotton planter… It needed a man of the border." Twain, himself a son of Hannibal, Missouri, put his finger on something important, even decisive, in the future president's life. Raised first among poor white Southerners, transplanted with his family to Indiana and then Illinois, Lincoln experienced more variety of ordinary American life in his early years than most people of his era experienced in their lifetimes.

He was born on February 12, 1809, in a rural cabin in Hardin County, where about 1,000 slaves lived among 7,000 inhabitants at large. Slaves were transported north and south along the nearby Ohio River or on commercial roads. Slavery was a grim but accepted fact of life. The white population generally agreed that whatever their other political differences, only one thing could be worse: free blacks, whose migration into the state was forbidden by law. Viewed as a potential threat, they could never be citizens. Early in the century, not even most abolitionists could imagine blacks and whites living and working together on anything like an equal basis, even if thousands of free blacks already lived and worked in many places across the South and North. For those who did not regard slavery as just and eternal, a massive return to Africa was thought to be the only true solution.

Lincoln's parents considered themselves firmly opposed to slavery. The family joined a breakaway Baptist church congregation that rejected the idea of anyone degraded to less than human status. What larger family legacy did young Abe inherit? The Lincolns can be traced back at least to eighteenth-century Berks County, Pennsylvania, where Quaker disapproval of slavery was common. His grandmother had grown up in the faith until her marriage to a non-Quaker prompted the local Friends Meeting to exclude her, following standard practice. An ancestor named Mordecai Lincoln, who had come to Pennsylvania from Massachusetts in 1720, built one of the first iron forges in the region and later served as a public official. Selling his share in the business, he moved to a farm and started a family. He and his wife had a son named Abraham Lincoln—grandfather of the future president--who married a woman from a neighboring family named Anne Boone. A first cousin of Daniel Boone, Anne was the "excluded" Quaker.

The Boones and the Lincolns parted ways, the Boone family settling in North Carolina, and Abraham and a brother moving to Virginia and then Kentucky. President Lincoln would frequently comment on his many cousins left behind in the Virginia Commonwealth—the home of Robert E. Lee, Stonewall Jackson, and other Confederate leaders who disliked slavery but dedicated themselves to defending their home state against the North.

Lincoln's ancestry thus included another important connection with American history and folklore. Daniel Boone, whose real and fictional adventures have been celebrated for more than two centuries, was already a major national hero during Abe's childhood, hailed as a "natural man," liberated from European affectations and limitations. Boone epitomized the free human spirit made possible by the frontier, where newly arrived (white) pioneers carved a new world out of the wilderness, facing all the dangers and adventure of encountering Indians, bears, cougars and other threats hiding in the virgin forests. Spending the last part of his life in unsettled Missouri, Daniel Boone became the original "Western" hero, clad in buckskin and wrestling bears in the most commercially popular adventure story of the expanding country.

The saga of Daniel Boone himself, according to scholars, also marked the beginning of the literary "tall tale"—a Lincoln staple. Until that time, stories and sayings of the frontier had mixed old English, Scottish and Irish folklore (the first thunder in spring wakes the snakes, birds and hens singing in the rain indicate good weather ahead, and so on); warnings about bad personal behavior ("if you sing before breakfast, you will cry before night"); and common expressions ("as welcome as flowers in May").

New tall tales and sayings were born on the frontier and began appearing in weekly and monthly newspapers appearing in the 1820s-30s. The "Humor of the Old Southwest," as it was called, described men and women who were larger than life and often too violent for anything that resembled settled society. They lived hard, died young, and fought each other at least as often as they fought "wild Indians," telling jokes and stories about themselves and the wilderness around them. In one story Lincoln liked to tell, a wife who comes across her husband fighting a bear, perhaps to the death, shouts her encouragement, "Go It, Husband! Go It, Bear!" The same wife, or someone like her, reputedly carried a small bag of eyes that she tore out of the heads of women rivals. For the semi-mythic male of the Old Southwest, an average meal consisted of pounds of meat and vegetables—perhaps an entire hog—washed down with jugs of applejack and gallons of coffee, providing the nourishment needed for all the adventures in a lifetime as brilliant and brief as a lightning-strike. Abe Lincoln, from his teens to the end of his life, was famous for telling the wildest, most imaginative stories and jokes, usually to make a point, often just for fun, but always with a straight face.

Physically oversized, Lincoln was also a champion wrestler and runner along the settled edge of the frontier. Like mythical characters, he was larger than life. At 6'4", he was taller than almost anyone he met and the tallest president in US history. Upon his death, the famed poet James Russell Lowell ended a poem about Lincoln by calling him the "new birth of our new soil, *the first American*." In him, as Lowell saw it and others agreed, the American character had crystallized; it was no longer an extension of European life, European thinking, and the European spirit.

At the same time, however, many of Lincoln's own stories expressed a set of morals different from those of the Old Southwest, a subtle repudiation of the senseless cruelty across large parts of the frontier. In this, Lincoln was far apart from Daniel Boone and closer to another legendary figure who was very real: Johnny Appleseed.

Born John Chapman in Massachusetts in 1774, Chapman joined the Swedenborgian church—based upon the wide-ranging ideas and writings of Swedish theologian, scientist, and pacifist Emanuel Swedenborg— and took to the frontier with just a sack of apple seeds. Johnny walked thousands of miles in his bare feet, slept mostly on the ground or in hollow logs, refused to kill any animal, and survived on fruits and nuts. He supplemented his diet, especially in winter, with meals offered by new and old friends among frontier settlers. He preached love and kindness wherever he went, westward past the Ohio territory into Indiana, where he died in 1845. His seeds were sown mainly to grow apples for cider and then hard cider, a popular alcoholic beverage on the frontier.

Abe Lincoln, never known to write or speak of Johnny Appleseed, carried more than a little bit of Johnny within him. Although he could bring nearly any young man his age to the ground and did, at times, hold his ground against a mob, Lincoln swore that he did not have the heart to shoot any animal larger than a turkey. He took no joy in bloodshed. He had the "mind of a child," according to a friend, and was incapable of intentional cruelty. Abe and John Chapman were alike in their fearlessness, but both saw themselves in the hands of the Almighty. They believed in the essential goodness of people, the greatness of human possibility in America, and the mystery of God beyond the dogmatic beliefs of mainstream churches.

Poet Stephen Vincent Benet, writing *John Brown's Body* (1928), one of the book-length poems about US history to reach popular audiences in the twentieth century, described the sixteenth president in simple terms:

Lincoln, six feet one in his stocking feet,
The lank man, knotty and tough as a hickory rail
Whose hands were always too big for white-kid gloves
Whose wit was a coonskin sack of dry tall tales
Whose weathered face was homely as a plowed field…

Abe Lincoln was born to be the stuff of legend.

YOUNG ABE

The Lincolns, taking in the frontier world around them, were part of a considerable population of settlers—white, English-speaking, and Protestant—that actually moved with the frontier. This was not the Wild Frontier of Daniel Boone, where aging pioneers had loved the freedom of open spaces and mourned the coming of civilization, but the agricultural frontier in motion, killing or pushing out Native American peoples as they went.

We can only wonder about young Abe Lincoln's fate if his family had not moved across the river to Indiana and then to Illinois. It was a move or series of moves that thousands of other families were making at the time. Within a generation, they created new communities by clearing woods and raising crops and farm animals to load on barges and sell elsewhere, or buying manufactured goods from the east. In legend if not always in fact, neighbors came together to share goods and raise barns for newcomers.

Lincoln recalled very little from his Kentucky life beyond what he described as "stinted living"—the crude cabins and near-poverty of his own family and neighbors—along with a few boyhood adventures. Then his life changed. Remembering himself at the age of eight, shortly after the family moved to Indiana, he experienced life "in an unbroken forest" for the first time. Oversized and strong for his age, he carried an axe that he swore he had used almost every day for fifteen years, putting it down only during plowing and harvesting seasons. He had had a little schooling in Kentucky and got a bit more in Indiana, although the teachers were barely literate themselves. "I do think," he recorded later, "that the aggregate of all my schooling did not amount to one year." He made his own education, then and later, often at night with the poorest lighting. As a boy, he wrote a verse in his copybook that reflected the self-deprecating humor he would become known for:

Abraham Lincoln, his hand and pen,
He will be good, but God knows when.

Was young Abe Lincoln eager to grow up? He remembered listening with great effort to grown-up talk, angry when he could not understand it, unable to sleep when he could not make out the meaning of adult conversation or when he got an idea in his head and struggled to put it into his own language. The loss of his mother Nancy, who died suddenly from the "milk disease"—milk turned poison by plants the cow had eaten—when he was only nine, must have deepened his fears about the future and his self-doubts. So perhaps did the kick of a horse a year later that briefly seemed to leave him for dead.

The move to Macon County, Illinois, near what would become Decatur, turned out to be a turning point in Lincoln's life. His father Thomas had selected the location as a good place to farm, and they settled on land ten miles west of the fledgling village in 1830. A few years after that, young Abe (according to another story he later told) fell into the Sangamon River and was nursed back to health by a kindly neighbor, with a concoction of animal fat that included skunk oil.

Abe's stepmother Sarah had long encouraged him to read, and he thirsted after knowledge from a young age, both to "improve" himself for future success and for the sheer joy of learning. As a young boy in Indiana, he later said, he had written letters for illiterate neighbors and began devouring any books he could lay his hands on. He borrowed volumes from one person or another, reading about one subject after another, never satisfied. The Bible was among the first books he read, followed by

Aesop's Fables, Shakespeare's plays, and the literature of the day—poetry, fiction, and history alike. Among his favorites was the popular biography of George Washington by Parson Weems, who famously invented the story of the boy cutting down the cherry tree and unable to lie about it. Abe's father could not understand a child who wanted to immerse himself in books instead of playing outside. When Abe was a teenager, acquaintances enjoyed his lively conversation, jokes, and stories above all. But as a young man, when others would go off together for nights of drinking and carousing, Abe would head back to his room to read.

After a year of family illness, his father resolved to move again, farther west to Coles County. Abe, now twenty-two, went his own way, first to Springfield and then to the small riverside community of New Salem. There, with a job running the general store, he plunged into a life of local popularity. He was known for his sense of humor and kindly attitude, especially toward children, but he looked so comical and spoke with such a Kentucky twang that he attracted sympathy as well—and he knew it. Lincoln was a proven boatsman, handling a barge with the same combination of strength and agility that allowed him to wrestle with the best of the local brawlers. When he needed to, he could chop fallen trees with dexterity, earning a nickname much used in later years, the "rail-splitter."

He also became known for something that most potential officeholders would avoid: reading "dangerous" books. That is, the kind of books shunned by deeply religious or evangelical Illinoisans. Abe joined an informal circle of people known to be "exceeding liberal in matters of religion," that is, non-churchgoers or skeptical churchgoers who were willing to oblige their families but doubtful about what the minister preached. Constantin Volney's *Ruins of Empire*, the most heretical work on Lincoln's personal list of dangerous books, was also on the reading list of his free-thinking friends. The work of a renowned French philosopher, *Ruins of Empires* predicted the collapse of all religions into each other and the victory of reason over dogma, establishing a society in which "populations are kept quiet by being read religious tales." Only Tom

Paine's *Age of Reason*, a notorious atheistic tract, was considered more dangerous to Christian morals among most residents of central and southern Illinois. Another Lincoln favorite, Edward Gibbon's massive *The History of the Decline and Fall of the Roman Empire*, with its explanation of institutionalized Christianity as the cause of the "fall," would have been so difficult for the people of the area that they would have hardly understood enough to condemn its heretical contents.

Ruins of Empire had gained its most important American fan when Thomas Jefferson translated twenty chapters after meeting Volney in the 1790s. Then vice-president, Jefferson insisted the chapters be published anonymously, out of fear that he would be attacked as an atheist with his campaign for president coming up in 1800. Another American translated the last four chapters, and the book circulated among those regarded as skeptics or "free thinkers."

Although the Bible would remain the book that Lincoln most often quoted, probably because it was most easily understood by his audiences, he would not soon forget the group of like-minded young men in New Salem who discussed religion and other subjects, cracker-barrel style, in Rutledge's Tavern and in the village store. They had helped lift him out of frontier ignorance, while instilling caution about what he could or couldn't say out loud.

In 1834, according to friends, Lincoln wrote a small book about religion in which he expressed his developing views. It most likely contained the idea that the Bible was not the inspired work of God but written by ordinary men, and that Jesus Christ might not have been the Son of God but only an extraordinary human. Samuel Hill, a New Salem friend and miller to whom Lincoln reportedly showed the manuscript, was horrified at the implications for Abe and tried to persuade him to destroy it. Lincoln insisted that it should be published anyway, but Hill, believing it would ruin a bright political future, supposedly snatched it from Lincoln's hands and threw it into the fire.

Can this story be true? The evidence lies in letters from Lincoln's friends in New Salem friends and the testimony of a respected local teacher who later recalled that Abe had written something of his own on "infidelity." While he could tell jokes and make up parodies of Bible stories, Lincoln just as surely could have believed in an unknowable destiny set by God's will, or what the Puritans had called Predestination.

This was especially important in the terms of slavery. Evangelical Protestantism of the time, like other forms of Christianity in the South, treated slavery as God's will. The dark-skinned "Sons of Ham," according to this view, had been sent to earth to obey their white masters, or in other versions, had been tragically trapped as necessary cogs in a splendid economic system that made America powerful and prosperous. Quakers abhorred slavery but were relatively few on the frontier. Freethinkers, growing more numerous with the waves of immigrants in the 1840s and beyond, had more radical ideas. As a young man, Lincoln edged toward anti-slavery views in ways that he kept largely to himself.

A trip south had likely reinforced these sentiments while he was still a teenager, before he left Indiana for good. He had taken a job with a storekeeper to move agricultural goods and meat to New Orleans on a flatboat that he and his partner had built themselves. He was stunned by the size of the city, its "incredible laxity of morals," and the savage cruelty of the slave market. Another trip two years later reinforced these conclusions. By the time one of his friends left Illinois a decade later for a business career in Kentucky, Abe had already decided not to live and work in a slave state.

Stories about young Lincoln and his occasional romantic experiences offer mystery on top of mystery about what was going on in his mind. One involves a girl his own age, the adolescent daughter of a family whose wagon broke down near the Lincoln farm in Indiana. He later claimed that he "persuaded her to elope with me," but twice the horse returned them to the settlement "and then we concluded that we ought not to elope." The story is most likely not true, the kind of comical, self-deprecating tall tale he told about himself and his uncertain love-life. If the tale were to be believed, fate deprived Lincoln of what would have been the ordinary existence of a farmer and his wife, raising a family and struggling to raise crops. The mystery girl, if she ever existed at all, disappears from his writings as his imagination turns to more important matters: reading considered useful for his future, including the history of the American Revolution and the ideals of the patriots. Much as he loved to entertain groups of women at social events with stories and jokes, he had other things on his mind.

At the same time, Lincoln harbored melancholy thoughts and dark dreams that his few of his friends and followers would ever guess. These can be seen best, perhaps, in lines of original poetry composed in 1844 that air the gloomy inner voice that crept out many times in his life. Like so many Americans of the time, Lincoln had absorbed the stories and poems of Edgar Allan Poe and, almost certainly, Thomas Gray's famed "Elegy Written in a Country Church Yard." But he found his own voice in writing about life's uncertainties, his sadness at human fate, and the recurring temptation to end earthly agonies through suicide:

Here, where the lonely hooting owl
Sends forth his midnight moans,
Fierce wolves shall o'er my carcase growl,
Or buzzards pick my bones.

No fellow-man shall learn my fate,
Or where my ashes lie;
Unless by beasts drawn round their bait,
Or by the ravens' cry.

Yes! I've resolved the deed to do,
And this the place to do it:
This heart I'll rush a dagger through,
Though I in hell should rue it!

Hell! What is hell to one like me
Who pleasures never knew;
By friends consigned to misery,
By hope deserted too?

To ease me of this power to think,
That through my bosom raves,
I'll headlong leap from hell's high brink,
And wallow in its waves.

Though devils yell, and burning chains
May waken long regret;
Their frightful screams, and piercing pains,
Will help me to forget.

Yes! I'm prepared, through endless night,
To take that fiery berth!
Think not with tales of hell to fright
Me, who am damn'd on earth!

Sweet steel! come forth from your sheath,
And glist'ning, speak your powers;
Rip up the organs of my breath,
And draw my blood in showers!

I strike! It quivers in that heart
Which drives me to this end;
I draw and kiss the bloody dart,
My last—my only friend!

      *   *   *

O death! Thou awe-inspiring prince,
That keepst the world in fear;
Why dost those tear more blest ones hence,
And leave him ling'ring here?

The same year, in a doggerel mood, Lincoln sent the same friend a twenty-two verse poem called "The Bear Hunt," a tale of the fading frontier ("When first my father settled here;/ 'Twas then the frontier line; The panther's scream filled night with fear/And bears preyed on the swine") in which the bear is seen running from men on horseback accompanied by dogs. After the bear is killed, the hunters argue over who will get the hide, when a dog suddenly appears. It seemed to Lincoln, in writing the last line, that the dog was like a lawyer fighting over a corpse. In this case, his poem was an example of Old Southwest humor, with violence, gore, and irony wrapped in superficial good cheer.

Had he never risen in politics, Lincoln might have been remembered as a minor poet who made his living as a lawyer. But there were also deep personal reasons for his melancholy verse. In addition to the passing of his mother, Abe witnessed the death of his first sweetheart, Ann Rutledge of New Salem, who succumbed to typhoid in 1835 at age 22. Lincoln, who had planned to marry Ann, rose from his own sickbed and rode out to visit her. He was sitting beside her when she died, and he fell into a deep depression. Friends found him walking by the river, mumbling insensible phrases. Years later, when he was looking for a wife, correspondence reveals that he could not do so with the same romantic intensity. He had come to see death as a commonplace thing on the frontier. He would see much more of it—tens and hundreds of thousands of lives drowned in oceans of blood—in the decades ahead.

Young Lincoln, before he decided on a career in law, was an indifferent businessman, partly because of bad luck and partly because he had other things on his mind. Looking for a means to support himself, he worked as the head clerk of a small New Salem store and then, borrowing money, bought into another store with a partner. They sold all kinds of goods, including calico cloth, hats, plates, socks, jackknives—and Kentucky rye whiskey. His partner snuck too many drinks from the whiskey barrel in the back room, and business went from poor to worse. Lincoln had spent much of his time outside the shop anyway, splitting rails for fences, building pens for animals, and learning to survey land. Becoming the local postmaster proved that he had friends but no gainful occupation.

LAWYER AND POLITICIAN

Lincoln's most important discovery while working in the New Salem stores may have been a pure accident. Then again, maybe his later "recollection" was just another sly story he made up about himself. By his own account, he bought a barrel of assorted items from a man passing through town, at a price so low he could not refuse. At the bottom, as he emptied it out, was a set of *Blackstone's Commentaries*, the famous law books compiled by an English authority a century earlier. The more likely story is that a lawyer in town loaned him the volumes. In any event, Lincoln dove into Blackstone's Commentaries and more contemporary legal tomes, including guides to state law in Illinois and Indiana, with his usual driven and devotion.

In his growing private library, he now had a set of books to pore over carefully and memorize as far as possible, a tool for his future. He was inching his way toward politics, trying to figure out exactly what he had to do, how he had to appear in public, and how to achieve his own vision. His first printed appeal to voters, in an unsuccessful run for the Illinois Assembly in 1832, joked overmodestly about himself and his background. He told a local newspaper that he was starting at a disadvantage because he had "no wealthy or popular relations or friends to recommend me." He would be happy to be elected, he said, but if he were to lose, he was "too familiar with disappointments to be very much chagrined."

Meanwhile, Lincoln was studying hard to become an attorney. He was admitted to the bar in 1837 and soon learned that the life of a country lawyer actually appealed to him. For centuries, a career in law had been considered a smart strategic move for would-be politicians. It became more so when European aristocratic families lost some of their control to the rising commercial class of the United States.

Illinois' Eighth Circuit, covering a wide swath in the central part of the state, consisted mostly of prairies, interrupted by rivers and woodlands. The white population had arrived relatively recently, much of it—like the Lincolns—from Kentucky and Indiana. Few settlers were prosperous, let alone wealthy, when they arrived. But the land proved rich with potential, fertile and ready for farming when the trees were cleared. This was Abe Lincoln's world. He studied with no one and apprenticed at no law office, although he had lawyer friends and was encouraged by a leader of the state's Whig party, who loaned him law books from his private library.

Young Abraham Lincoln was not exactly an idealistic attorney, advocating for a particular cause or class of people. He could defend a runaway slave one day and a slave-owner's property rights the next, according to the opportunities offered by paying clients. He traveled the dusty back roads of central Illinois in every seasons of the year, soaked in his horse-drawn carriage by spring or autumn rains, frozen in the winter, and soaked again by sweat and thunderstorms in summer.

It's easy, almost like watching a movie, to imagine Abe during those days. Outfitted with a new buggy, the first of his own in 1840, he traveled light—some extra clothes, a few books, a fold-up desk and small mirror for shaving. Arriving at a small town or settlement, he would typically walk around a bit, stop by the general store or sit under a tree, shakes hands with the people and share the latest news (newspapers being rarely on hand). Sometimes he traveled with other lawyers, singing, swapping stories, and discussing politics along the way. At night they would play cards or chess, smoke cigars, and drink whiskey (Lincoln politely refraining from the latter). Sometimes they wrestled each other or ran footraces or shot marbles, like small boys. Abe gained admirers wherever he went, especially among youngsters, because he could outrun and outjump the locals and his fellow lawyers. He also stood out in a bat-and-ball game called game called townball, an early form of baseball. He could always count on a good meal at the home of a friend or new acquaintances.

The boarding houses where he stayed were less than luxurious. Lincoln and other lawyers often shared a bed, sometimes three at a time. Bedbugs and fleas were common. Rain dripped down from tattered roofs, and wind whistled through gaps in the walls. Boardinghouse food was greasy and not very nutritious. In many towns, the lawyers suspected that their horses were being treated better than they were—or had less opportunity to complain.

Back on the road, prairie fires threatened intermittently, along with the usual dust, rutted or washed out paths, and the solitude of long rides between towns. Life on the legal circuit was lonely in a number of ways. Close contact with women was a rare event, except at dinners and parties hosted by townspeople (and visits with prostitutes by some of Abe's colleagues).

But Lincoln, in many ways suited to this life, seemed to love it. Physically strong, he was never heard to complain about the heat or cold, the living conditions, or the stress of his work. When he had time on his hands and no one to talk to, he turned back to his books, working hard to teach himself German and Latin or enjoying law books, novels, and poetry. Fellow lawyers would return from a night of carousing and find him in bed, reading by candlelight, working on a case or enjoying a book, cheerfully "improving" himself.

He embraced his solitude. Around strangers or friends, he would revel in jokes and exchange small talk, but close observers knew that he was revealing as little of his inner self as possible. He seemed always to be holding something back, rarely confiding anything intimate or controversial. In a crowd, his mind seemed to be somewhere else, far away.

Traveling around the circuit and meeting people stoked Lincoln's ambition for a career in politics. He was unusual in putting his legal work at the service of his would-be political career from the first moment possible. Although his initial run for the state legislature ended in defeat in 1832 (he later claimed that it was the only time he was "beaten on a direct vote of the people"), Lincoln ran again in 1834 and this time won. He was, most notably, the next-to-youngest member of the Illinois that year. It did not hurt his fortunes that he had volunteered for the Black Hawk War of 1832, a conflict forcing the aged leader of Fox and Sauk Indians, seeking to recover former settlements and hunting grounds, to accept reservation life with his people in Northern Wisconsin.

Lincoln himself saw no military action and, according to his own account, bled only when attacked by a swarm of thirsty mosquitoes. It was said that he saved a sympathetic Indian, who was enrolled as a scout in the state militia, from beating or murder by fellow troopers. Two thirds of the state legislature had volunteered to fight, and Lincoln probably felt compelled to join. He had never personally taken up arms before and never would again.

Lincoln was adroit as a young assemblyman, making close friends with the editor of the most influential newspaper in the state and moving quickly to establish himself in the elite circles of Springfield. His most important friends and clients included some of the emerging power brokers and business leaders of the region.

Key to the changes in Lincoln's world and his personal fortunes was the coming of the railroad. The arrival of train tracks, according to some commentators, marked "the end of pioneer life." Travel by horseback, at least between major population areas, became outmoded. More importantly, the shipment of goods, both agricultural and industrial, rapidly transformed living and working conditions. With the expansion of the railroads, Illinois doubled in population during the 1850s.

If Lincoln helped make the railroad—his votes on taxes and regulation in the state legislature greatly advanced the Illinois Central—the railroad also made him. In hardly more than a generation, Illinois went from an almost unsettled frontier state to a thriving agricultural center with at least one nationally important city of its own. Lincoln was at the right place at the right time, full of energy and ambition to take advantage of the rapid changes taking place around him.

He made a splash with a series of high-profile cases and, just as important to his future, he learned greatly from the thousands of people he met along the way. In every county where he worked, he met the key merchants and leading lawyers, building his network and establishing his reputation. He created alliances and cultivated personal friendships, not only among people who shared his views on slavery and other issues, but also among people who disagreed with his positions but were impressed by his energy, determination, and affable character. He sharpened his Kentuckian storytelling style, much the way Mark Twain did on Mississippi River steamboats. Instead of writing out his stories and developing them as fiction, Lincoln polished them as anecdotes, tall tales, and "shaggy dog stories" with no ending in sight. Even people bitterly hostile to his views could be won over by his personality. Or driven crazy by it.

With his down-home charm and winning personality, Lincoln could favor the railroads in many of his legal cases (and later, even more effectively, in the Illinois state legislature) without provoking the rage that many ordinary citizens felt at the railroads' abuse of landowners, small towns, and their own employees. Lincoln occasionally defended individuals and towns against the railroad, if mainly against the St. Louis, Alton & Chicago Company rather than the powerful Illinois Central. And while the railroads offered Lincoln opportunities as a young lawyer and legislator, they would prove important to him in a larger sense as the engines of progress.

From the outset, Lincoln developed his political positions with particular care. In his first notable speech to the Illinois state legislature, in January, 1837, he defended the state bank against its Democratic critics whose devotion to President Andrew Jackson and their own instincts prompted them to resist financial authority. If the bank's politically influenced examiners were willing to harm the wealthy classes, Lincoln argued, they could not do so successfully. The fate of the "unsuspecting farmer and mechanic" would be undermined, even destroyed, along with the value of the currency. In defending "persons and property," Lincoln stood up for the worthy poor, or at least claimed to. Favoring tax-supported, state-aided development projects of various kinds while fending off Democrats who claimed to represent the common man, Lincoln knew just what he was doing.

Although he was a young man headed for success, something dark still haunted him. Courting a young woman, knowing he needed a wife, brought out the shadows rather than dispelled them. After Ann Rutledge's death, Lincoln seemed to have little time for women, although he was widely regarded as friendly, almost flirtatious, in mixed company and was always full of amusing stories. To friends and acquaintances, he was a loner who either didn't mind being alone or was unable to be different. His on-again, off-again courtship of Mary Todd, finally culminating in marriage, brought out many negative feelings about himself but offered the compensation of a home with children that he loved dearly.

Todd was the daughter of the president of the Bank of Kentucky in Lexington; the family was well-to-do and owned slaves. Thanks to her intelligence and vitality, not to mention her sharp tongue, Mary was quick to become the center of attention at social gatherings. She left home for Illinois at age twenty after a dispute with her stepmother and lived with a sister in Springfield, the new state capital. Before leaving Kentucky, however, she is said to have told a friend that someday she would be the wife of a president of the United States.

MARY TODD

Lincoln and Todd met for the first time in December, 1839, two months after her arrival in Springfield. They were engaged to be married a year later. The relationship was not easy for Todd, however, as Lincoln was chronically melancholy as well as too busy for many of the parties she wanted to attend with him. Uncertain in his own mind and unable to write her a letter breaking off the engagement, he told her in person that he did not love her—and then took a crying Mary into his arms. Todd responded to the disappointment with a succession of undefined illnesses, probably making things worse with patent medicines (most containing alcohol, some containing opiates). The announced wedding day, New Year's 1841, passed without ceremony. Lincoln spent his time in the legislature instead, as he did nearly every day for months to come. He also grew more depressed.

The depression became so severe that he could hardly bear the pressure. It was a return to the dark mental state that Lincoln battled intermittently through much his life. In late 1841 and early 1842, he sought medical assistance and took a variety of "cures," from patent medicines to cold baths. He sometimes felt so suicidal that friends felt compelled to take sharp objects away him. And when he pronounced himself the "most miserable man who ever lived," he was not feigning the agony. He saw disaster all around and blamed himself for more than his share. He suffered treatments as extreme as any available at the time, including a nearly poisonous dose of a mercury compound intended to bring on fever, chills, and vomiting.

In the midst of all this, he reluctantly agreed to a duel with a political enemy named James Shields, who took offense at something Lincoln had written about him and issued the challenge. Duels to the death were a common way of settling disputes at the time, especially in the South, but they were illegal in Illinois. The two rivals took up broadswords at Bloody Island, Missouri, on September 22, 1843. At the last moment, they withdrew from the fight, shook hands, and road the ferry back together. Lincoln later told friends that when a representative of his opponent asked what weapons he would choose, Abe had answered "How about cow-dung at five paces?"

Six weeks later, Lincoln was married. He had averted death by broadsword and at long last seemed to come out of depression. Although two depressive personalities make poor prospects for marital happiness, the man who needed a wife and the woman who wanted a husband had settled upon each other. Abe, always busy, would neglect her for days, weeks, or even months at a time. Mary, frequently exasperated at her husband's conduct, let him know just how she felt and spent more on clothes and home furnishings than she knew he would want. She reveled in Springfield society, while Abe interested himself mostly in books and ideas. Unlike many other powerful men, he never pursued other women, kept no mistresses, and showed no sign of such temptations. Guilt, especially at not spending more time with the sons Mary bore in the following years, now seemed to dominate his dark moods at home and on the road.

Any reader of history is compelled to wonder how an obscure lawyer from a remote prairie state could imagine himself becoming president, and how his wife could proudly share the ambition. According to Carl Sandburg, casual acquaintances in the 1840s might already see in Lincoln a shrewd and calculating lawyer-politician. But they might just as easily see him as an awkward and frequently depressed man seeking a secure place for himself; or again as containing some mixture of moods and behaviors beyond easy reckoning. The real truth, if any exists, is not obvious, and looking at the evidence offers no proof for any particular point of view. Not a military hero, not a man of wealth or privilege, Lincoln had no clear advantages over thousands of other men in his rise to the top. One can only say that he was right for the time and seemed to sense it, using all his shrewdness and natural gifts to build his political following.

How could a man so humble in the eyes of the Almighty, as he often told listeners, carry such ambition? We will learn more as we go along, even if the mystery is never fully solved.

Lincoln Takes a Wife

IN 1834, WHEN ABE WAS TWENTY-FIVE HE WAS ELECTED TO SERVE HIS FIRST TERM IN THE ILLINOIS LEGISLATURE.

HE BORROWED $200 TO SETTLE HIS MOST URGENT DEBTS AND BOUGHT A $60. SUIT...

LAWYER JOHN STUART WAS ANOTHER YOUNG LEGISLATOR WHO SOON BECAME LINCOLN'S FRIEND

BEING A *LAWYER* IS THE BEST WAY TO GET AHEAD IN POLITICS!!

SO LINCOLN BEGAN TO STUDY THE LAW, IN ADDITION TO WRITING BILLS, GIVING SPEECHES, RUNNING FOR RE-ELECTION, AND WORKING AS A SELF-TAUGHT SURVEYOR TO PAY HIS ROOM AND BOARD.

OFFICES OF J. Stuart esq. & A. Lincoln COUNSELORS AT LAW

ABE RECEIVED HIS LAW LICENSE IN 1836. THE NEXT YEAR HE MOVED FROM THE FRONTIER TOWN OF NEW SALEM TO THE BUSTLING CITY OF SPRINGFIELD. HE BECAME STUART'S LAW PARTNER.

LINCOLN WAS BUSY WITH HIS LAW CASES AND WORK IN THE LEGISLATURE— HE WASN'T AVAILABLE FOR ALL MARY TODD'S PARTIES AND CONCERTS.

IF YOU *REALLY* LOVED ME, YOU WOULDN'T LEAVE ME *ALONE* SO OFTEN!

DID MARY TODD'S RELATIVES WEAR HER DOWN, OR DID LINCOLN'S INDECISION CAUSE THEM TO *BREAK UP?*

I AM NOW THE MOST MISERABLE MAN LIVING...

LINCOLN HAD ALWAYS BEEN SUBJECT TO SPELLS OF DEEP DESPAIR, WHICH HE ENDURED AS HE ENDURED FREEZING COLD, CRUSHING OVERWORK OR THE DEATHS OF LOVED ONES.

...IF WHAT I FELT WERE EQUALLY DISTRIBUTED TO THE WHOLE HUMAN FAMILY, THERE WOULD NOT BE ONE CHEERFUL FACE ON EARTH!"

AFTER HIS ENGAGEMENT WITH MARY TODD WAS BROKEN, LINCOLN WAS ESPECIALLY GLOOMY.

TOUCHED BY LINCOLN'S PLIGHT, THE KINDLY MRS. FRANCIS, WIFE OF A LOCAL NEWSPAPER EDITOR, INVITED LINCOLN MARY TODD TO A PARTY IN HER PARLOR

BE *FRIENDS* AGAIN!

MARY TODD JOINED LINCOLN WRITING PRO-WHIG SATIRES FOR FRANCIS' NEWSPAPER. THEY WROTE USING THE SAME PEN NAME. MARY TODD'S WIT WAS SO SAVAGE, THE AUTHOR WAS CHALLENGED TO A *DUEL*... LINCOLN TOOK CREDIT AND CHOSE BROADSWORDS AS THE WEAPON.

WELL, NOW, ABE — JUST *SIGN* THIS AND WE CAN ALL GO HOME...

..."NO INTENTION OF INJURING THE CHARACTER OR REPUTATION"...

IF YOU EVER WANT TO MARRY ME, LET IT BE *SOON*...

IF YOU'D LIKE TO GIVE US YOUR *BLESSING*, MARY TODD AND I ARE GETTING MARRIED THIS EVENING.

SIX WEEKS LATER, LINCOLN RAN INTO MARY TODD'S BROTHER-IN-LAW, NINIAN EDWARDS.

THEY BEGAN MARRIED LIFE IN ROOMS ABOVE THE GLOBE TAVERN, RENTED FOR $4.00 A WEEK. WHILE LINCOLN TRAVELED AROUND ILLINOIS ARGUING LAW CASES, MARY TODD WAS LEFT *ALONE* AND *BORED*.

ON NOVEMBER 4, 1842, LINCOLN, AGE 33, AND MARY TODD, AGE 24 WERE WED AT THE EPISCOPAL CHURCH.

35

IN AUGUST, 1843, THE LINCOLNS' FIRST SON ROBERT TODD WAS BORN. ABE LINCOLN WAS AN EXTREMELY LOVING AND INDULGENT FATHER.

LINCOLN AND HIS FRIENDS IN THE ILLINOIS LEGISLATURE MADE A DEAL TO MOVE THE STATE CAPITOL TO SPRINGFIELD. NOW LINCOLN WAS EARNING A GOOD INCOME AS A LAWYER, HE BOUGHT A HANDSOME TWO STORY FRAME HOUSE NEAR THE CITY CENTER.

REFINED, ELEGANT, UPPER CLASS MARY TODD WAS ABLE TO RECOGNIZE THE TREASURE IN A CRUDE FRONTIERSMAN. AND ABRAHAM LINCOLN WAS ALWAYS DEVOTED TO HER.
BUT MARY WAS HOT-TEMPERED AND MOODY. SHE WAS TO BE BROKEN BY A SERIES OF TRAGEDIES.

CHAPTER TWO

LINCOLN THE POLITICIAN

L incoln's law practice and the personal journey that inspired in him the pursuit of personal contacts and gained him a wealth of political savvy set the tone for much of the rest of his life. It would seem unlikely that experiences in an obscure corner of American society, far from the major institutions and personalities that dominated national affairs from the East Coast, could create a political giant. But this very location, as Lincoln grasped, was to become pivotal in the middle decades of the nineteenth century. It was no accident that Lincoln's law cases and the importance of his clients grew in scope through his experience with virtually every kind of defendant and legal argument. He assisted many a poor client but also grew close to some of the richest men in the state and to editors of the region's leading newspapers. He also grew intellectual and socially, making his way toward eloquence and popular appeal.

The nature of American political life changed so sharply from the 1840s to the 1850s that even Lincoln, at times, must have been as astonished as journalists and other observers at the opportunities opening up for a new politics. Building the republic at its heartland and then saving the republic were certainly worthy goals, but it took years for Lincoln to find the issues that mattered to him most, find his voice, and make his way forward.

The crucial turn would be driven, sometimes subtly, sometimes openly, by the plight of African-Americans and the challenges posed by the institution of slavery to the founding principles of the republic and to its future. In his rise to prominence, Lincoln was especially fortunate in his opposition on this vital issue. Illinois senator Stephen A. Douglas, the state's leading Democrat and a prominent figure on the national scene, provided an ideal foil for Lincoln's articulation of the crisis and its possible resolution.

STEPHEN DOUGLAS

*   *   *

Abraham Lincoln grew into politics without ever ceasing to be himself. We catch a glimpse of the process in Decatur, a county seat in central Illinois. Chartered in 1829, the town mushroomed from 100 residents to 4,000 residents by the start of the Civil War. According to legend, Lincoln was attending a sod-busting event for a cousin in 1830 and wandered toward the courthouse, where two Democrats were addressing the crowd. Hearing what they had to say, he literally leaped onto a stump and launched into his own speech about the need for improvement in river navigation. This is said to be his first political address ever, reflecting his insistence on clear talk and direct answers and showing his talent for poking fun at unfriendly questioners. Both skills would be crucial to his rise in politics.

Lincoln had a genius for picking law partners and other contacts who could help his career. He made success in Illinois politics almost look easy, if nobody but he and his fiancée, Mary Todd, ever imagined that he might one day become president. Homely, enigmatic, and frequently depressed, he hid his faults and exploded into the spotlight, focusing his attention and energy on the potential of the Whig Party.

For Americans today, it is difficult to imagine that the Whigs elected several presidents, held power in a number of states, and sent candidates to Congress. It is even more difficult to grasp why the Whigs, never well-organized, rose so high and fell so quickly. Its demise in the mid-1850s marked the last major development before the modern two-party system took a firm hold—some would say death grip—on American political life. We need to return several decades before the Civil War to understand the change.

The Democratic-Republican Party of Thomas Jefferson, successfully challenging the conservative Federalists of George Washington's time, morphed into a very different body as the nation expanded westward, industries advanced, and the Southern slave system prospered. The Whig Party, founded in 1834, rose to prominence in the fight against the politics and personality of the "malignant tyrant" (as critics called him), President Andrew Jackson. Following the decline and division of the Democratic-Republican Party, Jackson embodied the restyled Democrats. Probably the most popular and undoubtedly the most controversial political figure since the Founding Fathers, Jackson presented himself as a war hero and a "man of the people" standing up against the interests of bankers, business leaders, and other powerful figures.

The truth was more complicated. A slave owner who considered slavery a natural system of economics and of population control, Jackson built his reputation as "Old Hickory," the commanding general in the Battle of New Orleans, the final major confrontation with the British in the War of 1812. (The war had actually ended while the battle went on, as news of the peace treaty did not reach the combatants in time). Presenting himself as the frontiersman's hero from his own region westward, then called the "Southwest," Jackson was elected president in 1828 and reelected in 1832. In doing so, he even won the support of workingmen and working women in New York State, swallowing up the organizations they had created for themselves, the first "labor parties" founded in the US.

Jackson believed in the unrestrained, essentially unregulated expansion of the economy and in the removal or, perhaps extermination, of Indian peoples standing in the way of settlement. As president, he directed brutal campaigns against native tribes that twentieth-century observers would cite for war crimes on a large scale. The grand dream of Jackson's Democrats crashed in the economic crisis of 1837, a stock market panic in which speculation on inflated investments—including thousands of slaves moved westward for cotton production—suddenly wiped out the paper value of much of the country's wealth.

Young Whig Abraham Lincoln saw the world very differently from Jackson. He accepted that rapid national expansion required the retreat of native tribes from an advancing white population, but unlike Jackson, he did not regard them as lesser human beings fit for disposal. The continued growth of the economy and the expansion of opportunities, in Lincoln's estimation, depended upon an infrastructure that only strong federal policies could make possible. Tariffs, imposed on manufactured goods imported into the United States, would benefit the North the most by far, allowing new industries to grow. In the South, largely dominated by Democrats, the result would be higher prices for these goods. The issue of slavery remained less certain for Whigs, although Northern factions of the party included both abolitionists and those, like Lincoln himself, who considered the system immoral but saw no easy solution. Whigs elected in the South, mostly in the border regions, had an economic problem with the tariff that would be daunting enough to threaten their power; the slavery issue would finally overwhelm them and the party itself.

Within Illinois during the 1830s, Lincoln quickly made himself the Whigs' leading strategist, campaigner, and organizer. His plan for state organization, right down to the most local level—city wards—was the map for future victory. Only a few years after he ran for office for the first time, he led the formation of a state convention system to nominate Whig candidates for office. He met regularly with other leaders of the new state party, wrote letters by the hundreds, publishing many of them in the local press, and placed the importance of party unity at the heart of his efforts.

Whigs had almost always been on the losing side of Illinois elections, which made Lincoln's rise in the party all the easier. Calling for a grand system of internal improvements to speed economic growth, he was caught short by the same fiscal crisis of 1837, and the state was forced to declare bankruptcy. With the revival of the private economy, however, Lincoln won reelection to the state legislature in 1840, behind the victory of Whig presidential nominee (and former "Indian fighter") William Henry Harrison. Except for a single term in the US Congress, 1847-49, this would be the last time Lincoln held elective office before becoming president.

These were radical times, however, with new dreams and ideas in the air. The "American Renaissance," a literary phenomenon unprecedented in its New World brilliance, took place mostly in New England during the 1830s-50s, with such luminaries as Henry David Thoreau, Ralph Waldo Emerson, Herman Melville, and Emily Dickinson establishing a truly national literature and a new ethical philosophy. In New England and western New York State (known as the "Burned Over District" for its religious enthusiasm), socialistic utopian colonies, in which residents shared goods and labor, were being established; some featured a "free love" philosophy without marriage ties. In Seneca Falls, New York, the women's rights movement was born at a convention in July, 1848. The "dress-reform" movement, or Bloomerism, hailed unisex clothing for women, and radical newspapers sympathetic to new social causes advanced a doctrine of "nonresistance," or what would be called pacifism in the twentieth century.

Like many of the citizens of central Illinois, Lincoln at first seemed be unaware of, or not especially sympathetic toward, such big-city or East Coast reform movements. But thanks to generous postal subsidies, newspapers and magazines were extending their reach. Besides, Chicago was not far away from Springfield and growing closer by the year with improvements in rail service. In 1848 and the succeeding years, Chicago and the neighboring state of Wisconsin became home to thousands of Germans fleeing the homeland following a failed revolution against the monarchy. "Free thinkers," unaffiliated with a church, formed political and cultural societies in many communities that revolved around the "Turnverein," or gymnastic club, and the German-style family tavern. Contemptuous of slavery, they established political organizations and joined abolitionist societies as well. They would contribute Union soldiers to the Civil War far beyond their numbers in the population at large and would form a faithful constituency of the future Republican Party.

Northern Yankees and German-American immigrants thereby helped raise the issue of slavery and persisted in characterizing it as the nation's shame and potential downfall. Lincoln could steer clear of the controversy for only so long.

THE SLAVERY ISSUE

Lincoln the lawyer appeared to be drawing away from the frontier life, but it would be more true to say that the nation's vibrant midland was carrying him along, with a contradictory culture of habits and beliefs trailing behind. Although the United States was developing its transportation, communication, commerce, and industrial resources with amazing speed, the pace of regional and cultural integration was not keeping pace. As new generations came of age, the heavily populated industrial East, the plantation South, the burgeoning Midwest, and even parts of the Far West were taking shape on their own, with beliefs, behavior, and even language variations unique to themselves. In particular, the differences between North and South that would finally result in Civil War were growing stronger by the year and ever more troubling to Abe Lincoln.

Slavery was becoming the central issue for the Southern states, less so but still very much for the North as well. Citizens around the nation who had never seen a plantation or had had any strong views about Southern practices were learning about the "peculiar institution" and forming strong opinions. Race itself was not as much on peoples' minds because only a minority of white people viewed nonwhites as suitable for citizenship, let alone equality. The roots of these attitudes lay deep in the history of the country and a small, nearby neighbor.

In the decade before Abraham Lincoln was born, an unprecedented slave uprising broke out in the French colony of Saint-Domingue (now Haiti), a relatively large island in the Caribbean. For more than a century, sugar plantations had enriched not only European merchants but the new American nation as well. Slaves and free mulattoes, together making up 90% of the island's population, gained few benefits from these riches. A slave revolution at the western end of the island, led by a former house servant named Toussaint L'Overture, overthrew the white regime in 1791 and at various times repelled Spanish and French troops seeking to invade the island and reestablish slavery. For the first time since Spartacus in ancient Roman times, a slave rebellion had shaken a society from top to bottom; unlike Spartacus, the slaves in Haiti won.

The trajectory of global society changed irreversibly with the events in Haiti, even if white rule continued for many generations. Peoples of African descent in the New World, far outnumbering whites in various plantation settings, had already been making many of the important day-to-day decisions on crop planting, harvesting, and transportation for several generations. This was especially true in the Caribbean, where whites frequently died of fever and deferred many of the decisions. (Responsibility for crops often fell to mulattoes, who became a kind of interim class with limited rights that were denied to black-skinned peoples.) In Haiti, blacks asserted their collective self-confidence, defying the stereotype of passive black savages and throwing whites into a panic. By the early nineteenth century, French and Spanish plantation cultures extending northward to New Orleans and beyond, sent to America thousands of formerly slave-owning Haitian whites fleeing the uprising.

The violence and bloodshed in Haiti terrified white Southerners in the US, who feared a similar uprising if and when the plantation system were to be overthrown. Organized slave revolts were rare and limited, most of them small conspiracies easily put down with force (though individual slaves succeeded in escaping regularly in some places). On the plantations, meanwhile, slaves created an autonomous culture "from sundown to sunup" (hours largely outside white control). In the minds of white Southerners, any hint of support for emancipation would prompt the slaves to rise up against them. Thus they viewed anti-slavery agitation anywhere in the US as a danger that must be suppressed by every means necessary. Abolitionists, still few in number in the US until the 1840s, mostly believed the opposite: peaceful emancipation was the only way to avoid a disaster. The ban on US participation in Atlantic slave trade in 1808, following similar British action the year before, raised the stakes for both North and South.

Economics told yet another story. Some historians have characterized the first four decades of the nineteenth century as the "ethnic cleansing" of the South, with Indian tribes slaughtered or exiled to the West, opening millions of acres to economic development through private purchase of what were now government lands.

Lincoln was still a boy when New York congressman James Tallmadge proposed, in 1819, to ban slavery in what would become the new state of Missouri. The Missouri Compromise of the following year would allow some new slave states to enter the Union along with some new non-slave states. The problem had not been solved, only put off.

Like most major political battles in the US history, this one had deep economic causes. With investors from Europe and the North putting up millions of dollars in hopes of high profits from cotton, more than a million slaves were shipped from the Upper South to the cotton-growing Lower South. "King Cotton," and the slave system to grow it, had become essential to the regional economy. Aggressive planters and their backers enjoyed unprecedented success as the center of Southern profits shifted, and they demanded the right to expand the system farther and farther west without restriction. They also demanded "free trade" without tariffs (or import taxes) on the flow of commerce, as some of their greatest profits derived from sales of cotton to Europe, especially England. Businessmen in the North, organizing a manufacturing economy, demanded just as strongly the expansion of their system of labor, based on wages (usually low). They believed in tariffs to keep the goods they produced from being overwhelmed by cheaper imported goods from abroad. These economic differences alone did necessarily point toward Civil War, but they did indicate that the economic interests of the South and North were increasingly in conflict, even as the nation as a whole prospered.

The election of Andrew Jackson in 1828 seemed to offer a way out of the dilemma. Because Jackson had the support of Northern workingmen, especially in New York City, as well as many Westerners, his Northern supporters confidently put forth the idea of a new protective tariff on textile products and iron, something that manufacturers and businessmen desired in order to protect the growth of industry. The South, it was hoped, would be satisfied with Jackson's racial policies and plans.

Compromise did not satisfy the South. South Carolina's leaders, following Senator John Calhoun—the vice-presidential candidate nominated with Jackson—responded to the tariff proposal by insisting that the US was made up of states whose governments could decide which national laws to obey and which to defy or "nullify."

To accept national rules, they believed, might mean one day accepting the abolition of slavery. The resulting Nullification Crisis of 1832 only threatened a real crisis. Jackson, like his followers outside the South, simply refused to accept Calhoun's constitutional interpretation. In 1830, for the first time in US history (and the only time until the resignation of Spiro Agnew over corruption charges in 1971), a sitting vice-president resigned from office. Calhoun would go on to become a ferocious defender of slavery within the Congress. In 1832, when South Carolina refused to collect the taxes and actually raised a volunteer militia to resist federal authority, Jackson asked and received from Congress the Force Bill, which expanded presidential authority to enforce the tariff, militarily if necessary. Jackson did agree to revise the tariff, making it less stringent, but other Southern states had already backed down from South Carolina's lead. The South could agree, meanwhile, with many of Jackson's other major policies, especially the Indian Removal Act, which drove Native American tribes (even those dubbed "civilized" for taking part in state government) to federal land west of the Mississippi River.

But politics were being reshuffled as North and South drifted still farther apart and Lincoln entered the picture. The short-lived Liberty Party came onto the scene in 1840, challenging Whigs and Democrats alike with a carefully crafted message proposing that slave states retain slavery but insisting upon an end to the spread of the institution into new territories. In Illinois, Lincoln the politician calculated that he needed the support of Liberty Party voters to continue his own rise. At the same time, the state courts of Illinois actually narrowed the rights of slave owners, declaring in 1845 that any slave brought from a slave state into Illinois was automatically freed. Lincoln himself, in his private practice, had not been so aggressive, sometimes defending slaves but at least once representing the property rights of a visiting slave owner on narrow constitutional grounds.

History caught up with Lincoln when, nearly four years out of state office, he won election to Congress as a Whig in 1846. In May of that year, under Democratic President James K. Polk, the United States had gone to war on the thin pretext of a border dispute against a badly weakened neighbor, Mexico. What Polk and many other Americans actually wanted could be summarized in two words: territorial expansion.

The Whigs, with a temporary majority in the House of Representatives but outnumbered in the Senate, responded to the declaration of war by passing a measure, actually an appropriations bill amendment, known as the Wilmot Proviso. Slavery would be prohibited in any territory acquired by the US in the Mexican-American War. Although the amendment failed in the House, the heated debate over this measure during the following decade reorganized the lines of American politics from Democrats versus

Whigs, with supporters of both parties across sectional lines, into parties based either in the North or in the South.

The reasons were obvious at the time. Most if not all Southern elites welcomed the war, essentially an adventure by the American military on behalf of land-grabbing Texans, backed up by the widely popular idea of national expansion—wherever land could be safely taken from any other nation. The doctrine of Manifest Destiny, proclaimed by a newspaperman in 1845, purported that the growing nation, in its Christian mission and economic power, had the perfect right to extend its boundaries and push aside or conquer lesser races in the course of doing so. America had been guaranteed by destiny or fate, perhaps by God, to become bigger and bigger as trails were mapped to the West Coast and new lands were opened to ranching, farming, the railroads, and access to all sorts of natural resources, including gold.

The Whigs opposed the Mexican-American conflict, however, even when volunteers (more of them from Illinois than any other state) rushed to join what appeared likely a quick, easy victory. Six months of fighting guerrilla forces inside Mexico proved this expectation false, and prompted brutal retaliation against civilians by American soldiers—rape, robbery, torture, and murder—that foreshadowed the US invasions of the Philippines and Vietnam in later generations. The occupation of Mexico City, the capital, brought an end to the war in February, 1848, but President Polk was enraged that the Mexican government ceded "only" the territory of future Texas, California, Arizona, Utah, and Colorado. Polk craved all of Mexico. Among those who resisted further claims were some leaders among the Southern slave states, who feared that so many non-slave, non-whites could not be successfully absorbed into a white-dominated nation.

Lincoln made his own case articulately. The extent of America's claim to new territory depended not upon treaties but upon the American Revolution itself, he said. "Any people anywhere, being inclined and having the power, have the right to rise up, and shake off the existing government, and form a new one that suits them better.

This is … a most sacred right … which we hope and believe, is to liberate the world." Sparsely populated areas of Mexico might be legitimately taken up for American purposes, he thought, but heavily populated areas already had their own private property and other rights. "I suppose," he wrote, that "no one will say we should kill the people, or drive them out or make slaves of them, or even confiscate their property." Nevertheless, later in history, property in the former sections of Mexico now belonging to the US would indeed be largely confiscated or taken away by other means. Former Mexican elites continued to hold property, here and there, mainly through intermarriage; Indians occupying what had been Mexican territory had no rights at all.

Regions and parties counted most in Lincoln's political calculations. The Senate had passed a Whig resolution describing the war as "unnecessarily and unconstitutionally begun by the President of the United States." Every Whig voted in favor of the resolution, every Democrat against it. Lincoln's first speech in Congress attacked the very declaration of war by the president, demanding to know the exact cause beyond logically empty, morally hypocritical claims to "advance freedom." According to some historians, the congressional rejection of presidential "war powers," crucial into the late twentieth century and beyond, began with the Mexican-American War and Abraham Lincoln taking a lead.

The Democratic majority back in Illinois railed against Lincoln as a traitor, even though he had voted funds for the army to fight the war. By the time the congressional session had ended, Lincoln openly declared Whigs to be the real anti-slavery party. He was mistaken. Within a short time it became clear that pro-slavery and anti-slavery Whigs could not continue within a single political entity, and the way opened to a new kind of party—the Free Soilers, based on the principle of ending slavery in any new territory added as a state. Defeated in his reelection effort in 1848 by a pro-war Democrat, Lincoln needed to find his way again.

Illinois, meanwhile, was booming, notwithstanding short-term economic crises, with growth accelerating from the 1830s to 1850s. It was also becoming more firmly lodged in the sectional divide that would make war inevitable. Burgeoning railroad construction brought Illinois growers and suppliers together with consumers in the East and abroad, while cotton was booming in the South. Lower Illinois looked more and more like a border zone, if not one susceptible to slavery, and one increasingly outweighed by the economic and political powerhouse of Chicago.

Each region of the nation, now more clearly defined as North and South, claimed to represent the true American nation, and each side had historically based arguments, valid within their own contrasting frameworks. The arguments shifted as Lincoln was becoming, first, a popular state-based politician, and then a national figure, shrewdly reshaping his opportunities and his rhetoric in the process.

Inscribed in the US Constitution, the "three-fifths" clause valued the actual number of African-American males, who had no rights, at only 60% in determining the congressional representation of Southern states. In other words, each thousand vote-less male slaves, counted for 600 constituents to be represented. In practice, the Democratic Party had also established its own internal rules, demanding that any party candidate for president must win two-thirds of state delegate votes, thus ensuring a Southern veto of any candidate—in practice, disallowing anyone considered bad for Southern interests. The South itself had few immigrants even by 1860, with a white population overwhelming English in origin and Protestant in belief. Rich and poor white Southerners alike were, in their own view, the "original" Americans; the North, by contrast, was "foreign" and becoming increasingly so. The determined effort to crush even the smallest signs of slave unrest with murderous brutality was, for Southern spokesmen, the defense of (white) *republican* values and the freedom to live in a republic superior to the inherited aristocracies of Europe. To survive as a society, they believed, it was necessary to expand slave territory, or at least that they *must* expand into a more national system based upon race principles.

Northerners—politicians and ordinary citizens alike—increasingly viewed the South as a threat, not mainly because slavery was immoral but because the "Slave Power" seemed determined to rule all of American society. Meanwhile, the escape of slaves from the South and the assistance given to runaways by abolitionists and free black communities in the North prompted Southerners to demand enforcement of property rights, the capture of the escapees, and, worst of all in the minds of most Northerners, legal prosecution of anyone who lent assistance. The Fugitive Slave Act of 1850, part of a larger congressional compromise, made these legal requirements official.

Abolitionism was far from strong in Illinois during Lincoln's rise to prominence. Elijah P. Lovejoy, a Presbyterian minister from Maine who published an anti-slavery newspaper in St Louis until its press was destroyed by a mob, founded the Illinois Anti-Slavery Society in 1837. There were few delegates to the founding convention from Lincoln's home region, and the state's attorney general personally organized a mob to break up the conveners. That same year, Lovejoy was shot to death while defending his newspaper office in Alton, Illinois. (His brother Owen, a future congressman, would become a firm supporter of Lincoln.) Unlike their fellow idealists in nearby Northern states, Illinois abolitionists had few political victories along the way to the war. If Lincoln had ever run as an abolitionist, whatever his party label, he would surely have lost his political career.

Therefore, Lincoln kept himself separate from any formal link to abolitionists, repeatedly denying charges that he had supported them or was part of their movement. Yet in Congress, after the House of Representatives went through a controversial slave ownership bill symbolically declaring the right of the (white) citizens of the District of Columbia to hold slaves, Lincoln sought unsuccessfully to amend the resolution to allow a future change in the law and then voted, with five other members, against the bill itself. As a protest, he and a fellow Whig added a ringing statement insisting "that the institution of slavery is founded on both injustice and bad policy," but added that abolitionist agitation worsened the situation and postponed a real solution. It was a modestly courageous stand, given the current politics of Congress. Lincoln repeatedly condemned rioters who assaulting abolitionist meetings and press but said little about slaves or free African-Americans.

Political unrest in Europe in 1848-49 had an impact on Lincoln that remains difficult to measure precisely, but an impact nonetheless. Historians tell us that the Lincoln who reemerged from political obscurity in 1855 was not the same one who disappeared from Congress in 1849. Not only did he read about the popular uprisings in Europe, he began to support certain causes with determination and enthusiasm. Thus he penned a resolution declaring, in the Illinois press, that good Americans could not fail to support "the right of any people ... to throw off, to revolutionize, their existing form of government and to establish such other in its stead as they may choose." Strong in support of German, Italian, and Irish efforts to achieve self-government, free of kings and aristocracy, Lincoln deepened his sense of republicanism as a global cause.

A new element of this cause, for Lincoln, was labor—the plight of the workingman and working woman. As a strong supporter of the railroads and the business community of Illinois at large, he had paid little attention to the other end of the emerging industrial society. But the failed revolutions in Europe offered different lessons. Repudiating nothing he had believed earlier, he came to see the rights of free labor as a measure of civilization's advancement. "Free labor has the inspiration of hope; pure slavery has no hope," he wrote in 1854. In the eyes of some, this was almost a socialistic expression, and for German-American workingmen in particular, it would be a most welcome expression.

Lincoln's eye on the world was a New York daily, *The Tribune*, read widely across the US, with thousands of readers in Illinois alone. Its founder and editor, Horace Greeley, was a militant Whig and an eclectic radical fond of abolitionism, women's rights, and assorted reform causes. One of the paper's most enthusiastic readers, Lincoln exchanged notes frequently with the editor on various points, broadening his knowledge in particular about the waves of radicalism sweeping European intellectuals and workers. Among the items he read were many of the hundreds of published dispatches of a certain young German writer in exile, named Karl Marx. One of the Americans living abroad and admiring Marx's writings, fellow *Tribune* correspondent Charles Dana, would become, on his return to the US in Civil War days, an assistant secretary in the War Department government, often directly in touch with the commander in chief. A quick learner, Lincoln was not afraid of sources considered radical or revolutionary. As a president seeking votes in 1864 from within the rising labor movement in the US, he would one day hail the formation of the International Workingmen's Association in Europe, headed by Marx.

THE WAR COMES CLOSER AND THE POLITICAL PARTY SYSTEM COLLAPSES

The Compromise of 1850, put together by Stephen Douglas among others for congressional passage, quelled the threats of certain Southerners to withdraw from the Union. Under the compromise, California would enter the Union as a free state, but the status of other territories seized from Mexico remained uncertain; slavery, if not the slave trade, was now guaranteed in the District of Columbia. Most offensive to Northerners was the accompanying Fugitive Slave Act, intended to stanch the flow of runaways and discourage the efforts of the Underground Railroad.

The legislation effectively made slavery legal in the sense that Northern citizens could no longer ignore the effects of Southern life. It drove forward the contrary idea of racial equality or at least black citizenship among those who saw slavery as morally wrong, while it impelled Southerners to grasp how unwanted their ideas of race were among many ordinary Northerners. Representatives of the South continued to appeal to Congress for redress of what they regarded as serious grievances, while condemning contrary appeals from Northerners as wrongful, "inflicting injury" upon their purportedly innocent selves.

In 1854, a runaway slave working in Boston named Anthony Burns was captured under the Fugitive Slave Act, and free blacks joined by white abolitionists fought hand-to-hand with federal marshals to free him. As a crowd of 50,000 looked on, troops oversaw his transfer to a ship that returned him to Virginia. Abolitionists determined to make another legal attempt to end slavery.

The Dred Scott case of March, 1857—in which a former slave who had returned with his wife from the North to Missouri was claiming to be free for life—prompted a Supreme Court decision with an unprecedented verdict. Led by Chief Justice Roger Taney, a former slave owner, the court ruled that no black person could have standing in the court because none could become US citizens. Only once previously had the Supreme Court overruled Congress (concerning the Missouri Compromise). And no state, even those who freed African Americans, could defend them from federal claims: the American "community" was purely white. Lincoln later called the Dred Scott decision a "burlesque" of judicial wisdom.

The ruling seemed to make Stephen Douglas' compromise, allowing territories to choose freedom, an impossible solution. The court's decision also delivered the real death blow to the remnants of the two-party system still operating in the 1850s. The Whigs could not survive the division between Northern and Southern factions. Nor could the Democrats, under heavy influence from both sides, compete with a new emerging force: the Republicans. Lincoln found himself constantly maneuvering, usually seeking to avoid isolation but also lining up potential allies for the fights ahead. Things had changed so remarkably by 1856 that Lincoln placed himself prominently in the new Republican Party, founded two years earlier in Ripon, Wisconsin.

The Kansas-Nebraska Act of 1854, proposed by Stephen Douglas to secure national unity, compelled the North to accept slavery in existing slave states and in prospective states with popular support of the institution. The new legislation had the inevitable side effect of repealing the Missouri Compromise, under which no slavery would be allowed farther north. It compelled Southerners, meanwhile, to accept several prospective Northern states almost certain to be anti-slavery. Slavery advocates and opponents both rushed into the Kansas Territory, with bloody results. Abolitionist John Brown and his followers conducted violent raids on pro-slavery settlers that resulted in shooting deaths.

Lincoln may have been half-jesting when he wrote later that he had been "losing interest in politics when the repeal of the Missouri Compromise aroused me again." That is, moving past his congressional defeat, he had found a way to go forward. More than that, he began to think that the emerging national crisis demanded a leader such as himself. He probably never really lost interest, but was awaiting a new opening. Now it was getting closer. His logic crystallized, in important ways, when he condemned Douglas for breaking with the intent of the Founding Fathers to limit slavery to existing states. The defense of the Declaration of Independence and the Constitution, now applied to slavery, became Lincoln's rallying cry.

Lincoln had not rushed to join the new Liberty Party in the early 1840s, even while he craved the votes of the emerging anti-slavery movement. The party's leader, Salmon Chase, argued that the Constitution forbade slavery and that the institution was founded merely on state laws that required abolition. Like many others, Chase had been pushed toward a version of abolitionism by the specter of mobs rioting against anti-slavery newspapers and political figures in the North. As a lawyer, he won several cases in court with the argument that a slave's "right" to private property was distinct from the generalized right to property, but the courts in several Northern states, including Illinois, leaned toward restriction of slavery in one way or another. Lincoln found himself as a lawyer during the 1840s arguing for slaves' rights, but on narrow constitutional grounds. These cases, however, may have prompted his first hard thinking on the future of slavery in general. Under his foremost legal proposal, delivered in a message to Congress in 1848, all slaves born in Washington, D.C. after 1850 would have been granted "apprentice" status. When they reached adulthood, they would automatically gain their freedom—unlike older slaves, who faced no such happy prospect unless their owners freed them, in which case the federal government would pay compensation. The resolution failed.

Neither abolitionists nor Southerners saw any reason to agree to a process of gradual emancipation, and for the next two years, Lincoln went virtually silent on the issue of slavery. Out of office with the adjournment of Congress, he had nothing to gain by reexamining his own views, and no further likely prospect of becoming an influential figure in American life anyway. He despaired of any peaceful resolution to slavery, declaring "the problem is too mighty for me."

Yet he finally found his voice. In his famed Peoria Speech, held in that central Illinois city in October, 1854, he plunged nearly to the heart of the issues. It was the longest speech he ever gave; he provided the press a 17,000-word transcript. Claiming a foundation in the Declaration of Independence and the tradition of Thomas Jefferson, he declared the legacy of the American Revolution a "civil religion" and argued that the proclamation of freedom in that era was a destiny to be realized.

Lincoln's views on slavery had been evolving inconsistently during the early 1850s, in part because he hoped to hold the Whig Party together as long as possible around a national economic policy, and in part because he feared the deepening national division. But now his heart was moved, or he was motivated by shifting politics, to make clear his abhorrence of slavery itself. "As labor is the common burden of our race," he wrote in 1854, "that so the effort of some to shift their share of the burden onto the shoulders of others is the great durable curse of the race. Originally a cure for transgression upon the whole race, when, as by slavery, it is concentrated on a part only, it becomes the double-refined curse of God upon His creatures."

In Stephen Douglas, Lincoln found a perfect opponent whose views he could assault, while spelling out his own more clearly. As he explained in the famed debates of 1858, slavery for Lincoln was a moral ill, and slaves had every right to constitutional protection. Nor they could not be sent back to Africa, cast away without resources; the vast majority of American whites would not agree to do so anyway. So Lincoln fell back on the historic ban on the slave trade as the best reason to ban slavery in the territories certain to become states. In what scholars call the most developed essay of Lincoln's life before his presidency, he ended with the glum thought that "our greedy chase to make profit of the negro" might cancel out the "white man's charter of freedom."

HOME LIFE

While Lincoln was preparing for the key moments of his political life, it is worthwhile to note, as his friends did, the course of his marriage and domestic life. Mary Todd Lincoln, early in the relationship, imagined herself married to someone more successful and joked that her next husband would be rich enough to send her on a European trip, as husbands in fashionable circles did for their wives and children. She dressed in finery, wanting to be lovely for him at the balls and social affairs they attended. Yet she found him to be increasingly distracted, not only by the need to earn legal fees but also by the time he spent reading newspapers and other practices she considered neglectful. She would also bear the brunt of family tragedy: The couple had no daughters, and three of their four sons died before reaching adulthood—Edward (their first) died before school age of tuberculosis; Willie (Abe's favorite) at eleven from typhoid; and Tad at eighteen, also of tuberculosis.

As the 1850s wore on, Mary Todd spoke less often to friends and strangers of her husband becoming the nation's chief executive, though she did mention now and then what a "magnificent President" he would make. Her mood declined and her headaches worsened; she said to friends that she felt like nails were being driven into her head. She flared up at Lincoln sometimes but more often at the household helpers. In one of the stories told about the couple, Mrs. Lincoln quarreled with a young servant and ordered her out of the house. When the servant's uncle came to speak to Lincoln himself, he answered, "If I have had to stand for this every day for fifteen years, don't you think you could stand it for a few minutes one day?"

That Lincoln loved to play with his sons whenever time allowed may have been another source for aggravation on her part. As Mary saw it, he had the fun and she had the worry and the work. For one reason or another, her temper flared more and more frequently. He responded without raising his voice, and they endured each other. She declared him the most useless man on earth, unable or unwilling to help with shopping or housework or anything "except to warm himself and read."

When a new tabloid, *The Republican*, appeared around the house, Mary demanded, "Now are you going to take another worthless little paper?" Abe replied evasively that he hadn't asked to have it delivered— when in fact he bought the copy himself! In truth, Lincoln considered the newspaper an unnecessary additional publication, but he was not going to bother Mary with complicating details. The incident tells us much about the domestic life of the Lincolns. Overburdened with family tasks or annoyed for other reasons, Mary leveled satirical comments at her husband. Knowing that to respond would only worsen matters, he plunged back into playing with the boys, legal and political work, or leisure reading.

Mrs. Lincoln had none of the complaints that many other women of the era could make about their husbands. He didn't drink, gamble, or flirt with other women. She defended him as generous with the money they did have. And if he was not the "technical Christian" she would have preferred in a husband, and even if he did not attend church with her, she saw him as "a religious man" with "poetry in his nature." Meanwhile, between caring for their sons and managing a household, she kept up her fluency in French, reading new essays and novels when she acquired them. He appreciated that she was intelligent and that his destiny was tied to hers.

Only one other woman is known to have had a monumental effect on Abraham Lincoln's life: novelist Harriet Beecher Stowe. A minister's daughter, well-educated, and living close to Cincinnati where slave and free states bordered each other, she took up writing after the birth of her sixth child and the family's move to Bowdoin, Maine. In 1852, a popular magazine, *The National Era*, began publishing chapters of *Uncle Tom's Cabin*, and it was an instant literary sensation. The inhumanity of slavery, her description of the South as a "devil's workshop" (in the phrase of the day), and the portrayal of a Christ-like slave ("Uncle Tom")

Title-page illustration by Hammatt Billings for Uncle Tom's Cabin [First Edition: Boston: John P. Jewett and Company, 1852]. Shows characters of Chloe, Mose, Pete, Baby, Tom.

was eye-opening to the public at large. Oversimplifying in many ways, Stowe struck a nerve not only among American readers but readers around the world. Upon meeting her later, Lincoln famously said, "So you are the little woman who wrote the book that started this great war!" It was an exaggeration but contained much truth. Millions of readers had their first realistic look at slavery and could rationalize it no more.

POLITICAL DISAPPOINTMENT
AND THE ECONOMIC CRISIS

In the summer of 1854, Lincoln grabbed an opportunity to leave Springfield and his modest legal practice for the promise of a US Senate seat. An intimate of Stephen Douglas was about to end his term there, and Lincoln, running as a Whig, sought election by the Illinois Assembly. (At the time, U.S. senators were elected by state legislatures rather than by popular vote.) He miscalculated. Although Democrats were in the minority, the shuffle of political parties left him a few votes short of a majority. Lincoln threw his support to a Democrat with a better record on anti-slavery than his own, Lyman Trumbull. Neither Lincoln nor Trumbull was quite ready to join the new Republican Party, though both did so later.

The increasing practice of political "fusion," in which various parties or individual members lined up against the extension of slavery, suggested some major realignment ahead. Among Whigs, the debates over slavery caused division; among the new Republicans, they brought strength and unity. Lincoln moved swiftly to brush aside even the crucial economic issues that had meant so much to him as a Whig. He was the key speaker at the state Republican convention in October, 1854 and carried the day with eloquence; another of the main speakers was Owen Lovejoy, whose brother, newspaperman Elijah, had been murdered by a pro-slavery mob in Alton.

The first national Republican convention, held in Philadelphia in February, 1856, was even more ferocious, with former slave Frederick Douglass as one of the featured speakers. Mexican-American War hero General John Frémont was nominated for president, and some delegates looked to Lincoln as good material for vice-president. Though he finished second in that race, Illinois Republicans held him up as a rising figure in the struggles ahead. Lincoln campaigned faithfully and furiously for Frémont, speaking across

FREDERICK DOUGLASS

Illinois more than a hundred times. Democrat James Buchanan won the three-way race in the general election, with former president Millard Fillmore, nominee of the short-lived American Party (anti-Catholic and anti-immigrant) at the bottom of the list. A Republican won the Illinois governorship, another good sign for Lincoln's future.

In 1857, the collapse of burgeoning national investments, centered in Ohio, sent an overheated Wall Street into a panic of selling. Soon businesses were firing workers and manufacturers were shutting down. Underlying the panic as well were sagging agricultural sales to Britain, if only temporarily. The immediate effects were felt more intensely in the North than in the more insular and cotton-dependent South, where the chief consequences may have been overconfidence in King Cotton. On the other hand, the sense of instability gnawed away at American self-assurance. Perhaps, underlying the widespread belief in American progress, there was some great flaw.

It is important to place Lincoln's views of a prosperous, hard-working America against the collapse of the bank system. Influenced by European thinkers and their American supporters, such as Charles Dana, and compelled politically to speak more often about his own humble origins, Lincoln set out to understand and explain to the public why "free labor" must be the source of a free society. Southern ideologues, feasting their eyes upon the poor conditions of textile workers and others in the North, had insisted that wage labor was more heartless than slave labor. Not so, Lincoln told listeners. Ordinary Americans could lift themselves up by their own efforts. As he told a Wisconsin State Fair audience in 1859, most free labor in the North was "neither *hirers* nor *hired*," neither employers nor wage workers.

Was this a realistic view in the 1850s? Not in New York City any more than in the South. With the influx of Irish and other immigrants, rich and the poor in the North became more divided more with each decade that passed. But it could be true, at least in the eyes of a beholder in Illinois south of Chicago, even in Springfield where large new houses like Lincoln's own reflected the rise of common men and women through hard work and luck. Even strikes, which Southerners viewed as proof of Northern society's failure, Lincoln saw as evidence of freedom. Unlike slaves, who were in bondage for life, wage workers could stay at work or leave their jobs. Technological change along with geographical mobility would open new opportunities, as would trade abroad.

Later historians were to charge that Lincoln, helping bring railroad corporations and others into existence, was complicit in the creation of a society in which the very freedoms he celebrated were disappearing ever faster. It might be more accurate to say that, with his attention directed elsewhere, he took little notice of the acceleration of change all along but especially in his last years, during the Civil War. Perhaps he would not have believed in free labor as much if he could have envisioned another, less happy future ahead.

Seen from a different angle, Lincoln was aiming his ideas about free labor *against* the Southern arguments. The failed European revolutions of 1848, with their radical ideas, actually helped him reason out more clearly the way to combat Southern claims of kindly paternalism as a justification for owning slaves. Seeking the truth in the Declaration of Independence, that the pursuit of happiness is universal right, Lincoln argued that it "applies to the slave as well as to ourselves." This was a most radical idea, because American society would need to change greatly for that opportunity to become available for all.

Indeed, this idea was more radical than Lincoln himself imagined. Answering taunts by Democrats that Republicans wanted whites and blacks to be completely equal (even intermarry), Lincoln insisted again and again that the real issue was over free states or slave states. Nothing could move him from that position. The future of free blacks in American society remained unknown and unknowable to Lincoln, perhaps to be solved by some kind of colonization in Latin America, perhaps by return to Africa (though few black leaders desired either of these solutions). Never active in the abolitionist movement, never close to an African-American other than the several free black servants in his Springfield home, Lincoln could neither accept nor reject the idea of a multiracial, democratic future. The war ahead spurred his thinking, forcing him onward.

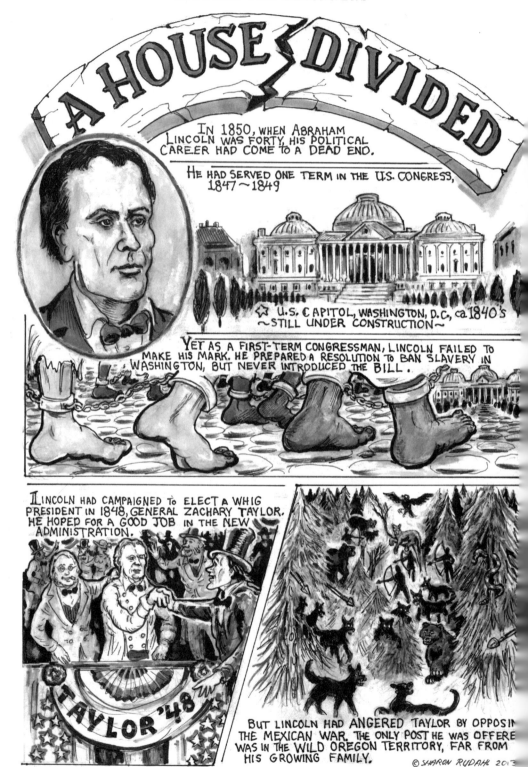

A HOUSE DIVIDED

IN 1850, WHEN ABRAHAM LINCOLN WAS FORTY, HIS POLITICAL CAREER HAD COME TO A DEAD END.

HE HAD SERVED ONE TERM IN THE U.S. CONGRESS, 1847~1849

☆ U.S. CAPITOL, WASHINGTON, D.C., ca 1840's ~STILL UNDER CONSTRUCTION~

YET AS A FIRST-TERM CONGRESSMAN, LINCOLN FAILED TO MAKE HIS MARK. HE PREPARED A RESOLUTION TO BAN SLAVERY IN WASHINGTON, BUT NEVER INTRODUCED THE BILL.

LINCOLN HAD CAMPAIGNED TO ELECT A WHIG PRESIDENT IN 1848, GENERAL ZACHARY TAYLOR. HE HOPED FOR A GOOD JOB IN THE NEW ADMINISTRATION.

TAYLOR '48

BUT LINCOLN HAD ANGERED TAYLOR BY OPPOSIN THE MEXICAN WAR. THE ONLY POST HE WAS OFFERE WAS IN THE WILD OREGON TERRITORY, FAR FROM HIS GROWING FAMILY.

© SHARON RUDAHL 2013

62

EDWARD DIED IN FEBRUARY, 1850, OF WHAT MAY HAVE BEEN TUBERCULOSIS. BOTH PARENTS WERE HEARTBROKEN.

MARY TOOK TO HER BED IN A DARKENED ROOM AND REFUSED TO COME OUT FOR WEEKS. SHE HAD ALWAYS BEEN HIGH-STRUNG, BUT THIS WAS HER FIRST BREAKDOWN.

LINCOLN SOLDIERED ON, WORKING AT HIS LAW FIRM AND CARING FOR HIS FAMILY. BEFORE LONG, A NEW SON, WILLIAM, CONSOLED MARY. BUT HISTORY WAS NOT DONE WITH THE LINCOLNS.

UNCLE TOM'S CABIN

UNCLE TOM'S CABIN BY HARRIET BEECHER STOWE, 1852 ~ A WILDLY POPULAR ANTI-SLAVERY NOVEL.

IN THE MID 19TH CENTURY, THE CONFLICT OVER SLAVERY WAS COMING TO A BOIL. BRITAIN OUTLAWED SLAVERY IN 1834. IN THE UNITED STATES, MORE PEOPLE WERE BECOMING CONVINCED OWNING OTHER HUMAN BEINGS WAS WRONG.

MODERATES, SUCH AS ABRAHAM LINCOLN, EXPECTED SLAVERY T END GRADUALLY. NEW INDUSTRIES AND ADVANCING TECHNOLOGY WERE BETTER SUITED TO WAGE WORKERS THAN SLAVES.

ABOLITIONISTS, SUCH AS FREDERICK DOUGLASS, WILLIAM LLOYD GARRISON AND SOJOURNER TRUTH DEMANDED AN IMMEDIATE END TO SLAVERY.

ABOVE ALL, LINCOLN RESPECTED THE CONSTITUTION, THE FRAMEWORK THAT KEPT SLAVE STATES AND FREE STATES IN ONE UNION OF UNITED STATES. AS LONG AS SLAVERY WAS CONFINED TO THE SOUTH, HE BELIEVED IT WOULD DIE OUT NATURALLY...

ca 1850
FREE STATES
SLAVE STATES
TERRITORIES

BUT IN THE 1850'S, TWO SHOCKING POLICY CHANGES FORCED LINCOLN TO TAKE A STRONGER STAND.

New-York Daily Times
KANSAS-NEBRASKA ACT
BLEEDING KANSAS
BORDER RUFFIANS RIGGED ELECTION

FINAL
Tribune
COURT DECISION
DRED SCOTT STILL SLAVE
CHIEF JUSTICE TANEY

©SHARON RUDAHL 2013

IN 1854, LINCOLN'S OLD RIVAL, STEPHEN DOUGLAS PUSHED THE KANSAS-NEBRASKA ACT THROUGH CONGRESS. THIS STRUCK DOWN THE MISSOURI COMPROMISE WHICH HAD KEPT SLAVERY OUT OF NEW STATES.

THE DRED SCOTT SUPREME COURT DECISION OF 1857 RETURNED SCOTT AND HIS FAMILY TO THEIR FORMER OWNER, THOUGH THEY HAD LIVED ON FREE SOIL FOR MANY YEARS.

BLEEDING KANSAS

HIRED THUGS, MOBS, AND MURDERS SPREAD SLAVERY INTO THE NEW STATE OF KANSAS.
RUFFIANS RIGGED ELECTION

ONCE A SLAVE, A BLACK PERSON COULD NEVER BE SAFELY FREE IN ANY STATE.

LINCOLN WAS ROUSED FROM HIS QUIET LIFE. HE GAVE FIERY SPEECHES ACROSS ILLINOIS, DENOUNCING DRED SCOTT AND THE KANSAS-NEBRASKA ACT.

"A HOUSE DIVIDED CANNOT STAND"— I BELIEVE THIS GOVERNMENT CANNOT ENDURE PERMANENTLY HALF-SLAVE AND HALF-FREE!

"THE LITTLE GIANT"
"LONG ABE"

IN 1858, THE NEW REPUBLICAN PARTY NOMINATED ABE LINCOLN TO RUN FOR THE U.S. SENATE HIS OPPONENT WAS HIS OLD ADVERSARY, DEMOCRAT STEPHEN DOUGLAS.

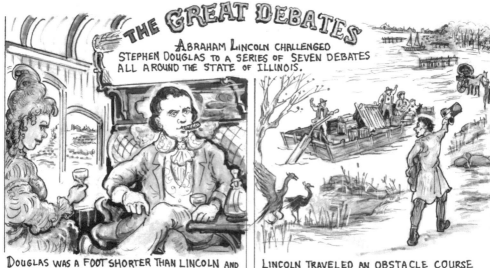

CHAPTER THREE

LINCOLN: POLITICAL GIANT AND WAR LEADER

braham Lincoln was the first American president to step into the role of military commander and direct strategy in a great armed conflict. To the present day, only Franklin Roosevelt's decision-making during World War II (until the time of his death) offers a near comparison. Lincoln's far-reaching efforts, the hiring and firing of generals, making sharp demands on some while leaving the fine-tuning of tactics to others, were agonizing and full of contradiction. Yet few doubt that the war for the preservation of the republic could have been won without his determination and guidance.

Lincoln's nomination and the presidential campaign of 1860 had signaled that the Civil War was inevitable. Whether a different Republican candidate—or a Republican defeat by one of the other two major party candidates—would have brought a different outcome remains unknown. Most historians would agree that the South had already pulled so far away from the North, drawing upon so many assumptions about an independent future, that the die had been cast. Lincoln entered the campaign knowing, despite his own words, that nothing he could do would alter the likelihood of secession. In his heart of hearts, he was already planning the military campaign ahead, possibly anticipating better than optimists on either side who believed the armed conflict would be brief and not terribly bloody. This time in his life seemed to be shadowed by premonitions, not only about himself but about the nation; he would be closer to the Deity than he had ever been in his life and would read the Bible more than he had since childhood.

Religion aside, Lincoln had prepared himself in a most unusual way. By the late 1850s, he had been advised to make the most of his modest frontier background. Increasingly, he recalled real-life experiences to present himself as a devoted supporter of an America that existed partly in his imagination and only partly in reality. Here, the land of opportunity (for whites, at any rate) was the land of the producer, of the small-scale businessman or farmer, of the young man who, by working hard and using his native intelligence, could expect to make a decent living and perhaps achieve a significant rise in status. Those who began in jobs working for others could soon, with a bit of luck, work for themselves. New inventions, the growth of foreign trade, and the expansion of white settlement, commerce, and mineral excavation across the nation to the West Coast—all of these together ensured prosperity, an escape from the miseries and oppression known to the great majority of humankind for ages.

Lincoln's imagined America, threatened by the values and ambitions of the Slave South, would be admired across the world for its virtues as much as for its wealth and power. Lincoln himself, in his rise to prominence, offered proof, or at least an example, of what this America made possible. He managed to set aside observations not only about the situation of non-whites in the North and the plight of Native Americans, but also the bankers and their stock manipulations that triggered the Panic of 1857 and the influence of railroads in push aside anything that blocked the rise of shareholder titans. Most of all, he managed to take the cost of the American Empire to its many victims entirely out of the picture—with the significant exception of slavery.

Lincoln's deep personal sincerity was never in doubt. In his last years, during the war, he spent several days nearly every week with the soldiers themselves, in military hospitals and the national Soldiers Home where they suffered. The sight of their devotion to him and to the cause of the Union allowed him to go on. His favorite soldiers were the Invalid Corps, the men who had been wounded too severely to return to combat and could have gone home with pensions, but who determined to serve in some capacity, mainly security duties. He was devoted to the selfless heroes of the republic, and, as he reached for the destiny awaiting him, he was becoming just such a hero.

THE LINCOLN-DOUGLAS DEBATES

For Lincoln the politician, the contest for the presidency in 1860 began in 1858. It was widely believed, at least by the time Lincoln died, that the seven famous Lincoln-Douglas debates, pitting two political giants across the state for weeks, had sealed the Republican's fate for anything less than presidency. On the other hand, the debates had situated Lincoln perfectly as a future Republican candidate. With his old motto "Once a Whig, always a Whig," he had written no less than several hundred, mostly unsigned partisan articles in his local paper, the *Springfield Whig* during the 1830s-40s. That time had passed with the disintegration of the Whig party, and now he was a Republican heart and soul—even if no one could quite identify, in all the competing interests and points of view, exactly what a Republican might be.

Ida Tarbell, one of the leading "muckraking" journalists of the early twentieth century, wrote in her 1900 biography of Lincoln that on opening the campaign for the Senate, Lincoln's famed speech, "a house divided against itself cannot stand ... this government cannot endure half slave and half free," was the most brilliant stroke of a political lifetime. He could not win over the support of those who sought to pay any price to keep the South from seceding, a price that Douglas was eager to have paid. Lincoln combatted the furious race-baiting of Douglas and, with deft arguments that preserved the devotion of moderate Republicans, made himself the only possible champion of the party's cause.

Douglas could not escape the trap that Lincoln had skillfully laid for him. Lincoln's small circle of tactical advisors, fearing too much controversy for their candidate, did not want him to pose the crucial question, "Can the people of a territory in any lawful way, against the wish of any citizen of the United States, exclude slavery from its limits prior to the formation of a State Constitution?" Lincoln shrewdly took his own counsel. If Douglas answered "No," he would lose his supporters in Illinois. But if he said "Yes," Southerners would never cast a ballot for him should he win the Democratic nomination only two years away, in 1860. The pro-slavery press indeed howled when the Democrat admitted that such laws could prevent a new slave state from entering the Union.

In the Illinois towns and villages that the debaters visited, publicity around the political questions alone might have been enough to prompt a good turnout. Taking no chance, Democrats arranged for a brass band at all the key stops, along with thirty-two gun salutes (for the thirty-two states then in the Union). Lincoln's entourage provided a stark contrast, with the candidate showing up on a veritable hayride, pulled along by working farm horses. The carnival atmosphere brought out patent-medicine salesmen, food vendors, jugglers, and the inevitable pickpockets. Newspapers across the country reported the debates. It was a grand example of American popular (political) culture, a real-life drama as interesting as any stage show, novel, or poem.

Thus did Lincoln become a political figure of national importance. Building on his staggering oratorical display of the past months in other states, all the way to New York and New England, a man less than handsome, with only one successful election to national office, had made himself the front-runner for the impending presidential race. Lincoln added substance to his lore by having an edited version of Lincoln-Douglas speeches published as a book almost immediately. He also confirmed, as did no other rising politician, that the issues of slave states vs. free states, while divisive for two generations, could not to be deferred any longer.

He had begun arguing against slavery on Constitutional grounds, leaning upon his own reading of US history since his young days. While he did not believe in full racial equality, he added, blacks were entitled to life, liberty, and the pursuit of happiness as articulated in the Declaration of Independence. If the logic of his argument seemed rather dubious, his presentation of ideas was forceful. So was the presentation of his personality. As noted by historian and 1972 presidential candidate George McGovern in his biography of Lincoln, the highest office in the land has probably never had a better speechwriter, ranking Lincoln with Thomas Jefferson far above modern figures who count on staffs to dream up their best lines.

Lincoln joshed Douglas that potential office holders seeing "in his round, fruitful face post-offices, land-offices, ambassadorships" and such found no such prospect in the rail-splitter's own "poor, lean, lank face." But this was true only because Douglas, for the moment, was much more well-known. Supporters of the fledgling Republican Party, at least the important ones, expected something in return for their support. Lincoln cleverly made himself the underdog, free of post-election commitments, while quietly lining up his money- and organization-men. Lincoln lost the race to Douglas in 1858 for assorted reasons, but mainly because the change in voting proportions of the Illinois state assembly had not kept up with the growing population in the northern region. It would have been sweet to win and join the Senate. But now was the time to look ahead.

Straight ahead, undermining any hope of regional reconciliation, was a major moment in American history that was sudden and unexpected,

JOHN BROWN

yet suffused with the highest drama. Within a year of the Lincoln-Douglas Debates came the raid on Harpers Ferry, Virginia. Abolitionist John Brown led twenty-two black and white men in an assault on the US arsenal there, hoping to precipitate a mass uprising of slaves. Brown had made no effort to prepare the slaves of the region, or to make good on his own group's escape. Federal troops led by Robert E. Lee easily quelled the would-be revolt, and the hanging of Brown himself was scheduled for the second day of December, 1859. A rather reckless figure who had led attacks on Southern sympathizers in Kansas a few years earlier, Brown was nevertheless apotheosized as a saint and martyr by intellectuals and anti-slavery activists across the nation. Slavery had now been deemed so evil, so intolerable, that the kind of violence visited against people of color for centuries now could be, with moral cause, directed against their white persecutors.

THE NOMINATION AND THE CAMPAIGN

Chicago was chosen as the site of the 1860 Republican convention, a momentous decision strongly urged by Lincoln's supporters. The unofficial capital of the Northwest and the newest American metropolis, Chicago by this time had a population of more than 100,000, as well as vast stockyards, docks for commerce on Lake Michigan, towering grain elevators, manufacturing plants of various kinds, and rail facilities that made it the agricultural transportation hub of the entire region. It was also a city of a thousand taverns. Chicago had a rapidly growing immigrant population that was heavily Catholic, Lutheran, or free-thinking. It was as unlike the predominantly Protestant, native-born population of "downstate" Illinois as could be imagined. By contrast to Lincoln's adopted home of Springfield, not more than a tenth of Chicago residents had come from Kentucky; tens of thousands came not only from Europe but also from New England, doubling the city's population in a single decade after 1850. The center of city politics was a hotel that could hold 1,000 guests. In May, they and thousands of others came to the city to nominate a candidate for what they rightly expected to be the very first Republican president.

David Wilmot was the convention chairman, and none could miss the symbolic significance of the man whose amendment—the Wilmot Proviso—had, in effect, divided the politics of the nation by geography. Lincoln's chief rival within the party, William Seward, led in early balloting for the nomination. But 40,000 non-natives of Chicago were reputed to be on hand for the rail splitter. The first two ballots went to Seward, but the future president triumphed overwhelmingly in the third. Even by this time, American newspapers outside the Midwest and those published abroad, reporting on convention developments, had trouble spelling Lincoln right.

His campaign managers cut many deals along the way, but the main planks of the Republican platform were genuinely popular, and not only for hard-core members of the party. The promise of homesteads for would-be farmers proved hugely popular, although in practice it would best serve those who could overcome various difficulties, including the ownership of much of the best land by the railroads. The adjusted tariff pleased former Whigs, and the promise of economic growth would aid everyone—or so the platform proclaimed.

Business leaders controlled the committees as well as the funds to pay for a vigorous campaign. But even with all the spending and promotion, pro-Lincoln "Wide Awake" clubs could not have launched the wildly successful torchlight parades and assorted events that rallied support without strong public interest and enthusiasm. The biographies of Lincoln that would grow to more than 1,000 by the end of the twentieth century already numbered nearly a half dozen before the 1860 campaign concluded! Already there was a readership because, within just a few months of his nomination, Lincoln had emerged as a major *personality*.

He was a source of fascination at home and abroad as a true "American type," someone who could have come from nowhere but frontier America, who talked and joked in a unique manner for a major political figure, and who could offer oratory as eloquent as any person on the planet.

The campaign rolled along, with Lincoln expressing himself in moral terms to an extent he had not done before. Wearying of being asked about economic growth, the Republicans' usual strong point, he told a reporter, "Pictures of mere industrial value of the Union make me profoundly sad. Is this the whole fruit of ages of toil, sacrifice, and thought? Does it result only in ... fops melted in baths ... and men grim with toil?" Challenged whether he could see any future for African-Americans, recent immigrants, and others presumed outsiders in the national destiny, he answered in the same high-minded tone: "Crowding to the shelter of [our nation's] stately arches, I see old and young, learned and ignorant, rich and poor, native and foreign, pagan Christians and Jews, black and white, in one land, harmonious, triumphant procession." It was a grand picture of the possible, happy future America.

By the early fall of 1860, still residing in Springfield, Lincoln no doubt appreciated how the Republican Party was taking shape around his message and through his efforts. His publicity campaign, conducted in those days mainly through newspapers, anointed him as the Backwoodsman, the Man of the People born into poverty and raised up by his own efforts, honest and even (at his age) "Old Abe," a veritable sage. Other newspapermen, including some loyal to the Republicans, squirmed at his stories of backwoods life and declined to retell them in print because they would seem uncivilized to sophisticated readers.

One of Lincoln's most intimate observers, St. Louis painter Alban Jasper Conant, who was working on a portrait of the candidate, recalled a quality in him that seemed to elude the welter of publicity. In the tales Lincoln reveled in, or substituted for ordinary conversation, said Conant, there was "some striking touch of nature, emphasized by gross absurdity, of such point and power as to elevate it above the level of vulgarity." These contradictions reinforced Conant's perception of tragedy and comedy, laughter and tears, at the same time sweeping across Lincoln's face. Perhaps those who observed him on the platform grasped this best. As Lincoln threw himself passionately into the expression of his ideas, the division between private and public figure disappeared: this was, simply, Lincoln.

Poor Stephen Douglas, running against an emerging legend, clung to mere remnants of a once-solid Democratic Party. In another age, not far behind and not far ahead (if Douglas had lived to the 1864 campaign), he might still have carried New York State, held onto the South, and actually won the election for the fractionalized Democrats. He was eloquent in his pleas to save the Union, half-slave and half-free.

Douglas would not endorse but could not entirely disown the unprecedented abuse Southerners in particular poured upon Lincoln— they called him the father of illegitimate black children, an ape, a mulatto, an idiot, and worse. Over the course of the campaign, Douglas seemed to shrink into a defensive stance, offering nothing new but an unconvincing picture of democracy of a limited kind, above all in race, preserved through compromise. Lincoln, by contrast, seemed to grow in moral stature. Douglas remained the safer candidate for large numbers of worried white Americans.

Lincoln won the Electoral College despite carrying only 40% of popular votes. Although he beat Douglas by a half million votes, his opponents together totaled almost a million more than the Republican ticket. Douglas won nothing in the South — John C. Breckinridge of the Constitutional Democrats carried the field there for undaunted slavery loyalists—and his vote was shaky in the Northwest, including Illinois. With the slightest change in the tally, however, Douglas would have tied Lincoln in the Electoral College. That would have turned the decision over to the House of Representatives, where the majority Democrats would be certain to choose Lincoln's worthy opponent. It was a close call.

Between the election and his inauguration, Lincoln shut down his

Springfield law office and prepared to take command of Washington, including the certain war ahead. He sold the Illinois *Staats-Anzeiger* (which he had bought years earlier to influence German-language voters in Illinois, but his ownership had never become public knowledge) to the paper's previous owner, threw some of his old correspondence into the fire, said goodbye to friends, and made arrangements to set out on his new life.

GENERAL WINFIELD SCOTT

He had been warned of assassination attempts. As a security measure, he delegated a friend and Illinois state official to meet the commanding general of the US Army, Mexican War hero General Winfield Scott, and gain his Scott's loyalty. The Virginian-born general, aging and unwell—not to mention too heavy to mount a horse—promised to take personal responsibility for Lincoln's safety and to employ every measure necessary. Nevertheless, an impromptu speech at the Springfield train station of the Great Western Railroad offered a classic Lincolnian mixture of determination and fatalism. Acknowledging that "no one who has never been placed in a like position can understand my feelings at this hour, nor the oppressive sadness I feel at this parting," he said. "Unless the great God who assisted [George Washington] shall be with and aid me, I must fail." Perhaps the old feelings of depression had returned, combined with a sense of the task history laid before him.

THE WAR BEGINS

The election results shocked Southern whites more than it surprised them. Widespread Northern sympathy for John Brown's raid and for Brown himself, martyr to freedom, had already convinced many Southerners that secession was altogether moral, as well as inevitable. In December, 1860, a state convention in South Carolina voted unanimously to secede from the Union. Six other states soon followed along, despite differences in some regions where slaves and slave owners were few. The Confederate States of America (CSA) had been formed. Some Northern leaders had believed that their counterparts in the South had been bluffing. Southerners were more self-deluded, apparently believing that the North would accept secession passively. They continued to ignore facts under their eyes: eight slave-holding states did not secede at once, although four followed later. Democratic President James Buchanan, still holding office, took no measures in response to the secession. It was all up to Lincoln now.

The president-elect, for his part, had doubts about the willingness of ordinary Southern white farmers to go to war. These people, many of them with a background similar to his own, had "too much of good sense, and good temper, to attempt the ruin of the government." He had a point. Some historians, treating the southern sections of Ohio, Indiana, and Illinois as part of the "cultural South," would estimate that 40% of this part of the South actually fought for the Union. In a border state like Missouri, a little farther to the south, Union recruits greatly outnumbered Confederate recruits—not to mention the thousands of Texans of German immigrant origins who joined the Union army. In the larger sense, however, Lincoln was wrong. Fear of racial uprisings, evangelical defenses of supposed Southern morality against the "foreign" ideas of the North, and the grandeur of Southern military *esprit de corps* guaranteed loyalty to the rebellion in the first years of the war, if not the last. Southern leaders going into the war believed Yankees to be cowards incapable of conquest, and many of their foot soldiers agreed.

The two capitals, Washington and Richmond, stood only 70 miles apart. Two new presidents, Lincoln and Jefferson Davis, faced some of the same problems, from the logistics of providing for troops to the stubborn reality of state politicians unwilling to sacrifice their independence in the name of the war effort. The similarities ended there. Lincoln wanted to call the shots for the invading Union forces and did so increasingly, as his generals failed to go on the attack during the early, frustrating years of the war. Davis relied heavily on his generals and, beyond them, a white population defending its own territory.

The Confederate capture of Fort Sumter, located on an island in the harbor of Charleston, South Carolina, set the war in motion in April, 1861, without a single Confederate fatality. Lincoln conceded tactical defeat, but set himself the larger task of holding the border states that chose to stay in the Union: Missouri, Maryland, Kentucky, and Delaware. The state of Maryland, adjoining the nation's capital, was a particular sore point. Southern sympathizers destroyed the telegraph lines from Baltimore to Washington, and the capital lost contact with Union states for nearly a week. Lincoln had the ringleaders arrested and held without trial, the first of many violations of civil liberties made in the name of national preservation. Kentucky stayed with the Union, though it served as a lucrative, illegal trading post with the South; Missouri became a site of hit-and-run battles, with an exiled Confederate government claiming what it could not control. Lincoln's victory in keeping these states from defecting was his first major triumph, and he knew it. Nearly half the white population of the entire South lived along the border, and more than three-quarters of the manufacturers. But Lincoln could not set his troops for the victory that seemed within reach. Blessed with thousands of well-trained officers and a handful of extraordinarily gifted generals, the South could outfight and outmaneuver Union battalions far larger in number.

On his political homefront, Lincoln had to manage the Republican Party, which was still new and still based on loose alliances, in order to manage the government. Liable to be swayed by a few dominant personalities, the party included several of Lincoln's high-profile rivals, whom he willingly drew into his inner circle and the cabinet in order to run Congress and the war effort. He won over the new Secretary of State, William Seward, widely regarded as the true leader of the party, but often found himself at odds with Salmon P. Chase, the determined abolitionist who served as Secretary of the Treasury. Despite their many conflicts, Chase made the decision to sell government bonds to wealthy investors and to print paper money in large quantities—centralizing national finance by barring state banks, for the first time, from issuing their own currency. This was crucial for the war effort.

Whether he meant to do so or not, by prosecuting the war, Lincoln was building a new federal government. The government in Washington quickly became so strong that it would never—and in terms of its new responsibilities *could* never—return the power it obtained during the war back to states, which until that time had been governed primarily by local and regional elites. The absence of Southern Democrats in Congress allowed Republicans to push through plans for the Transcontinental Railroad and for the Homestead Act, which offered 160 acres of public land to enterprising farmers and ranchers. Along with the formation of a Department of Agriculture, the Lincoln administration passed the Morrill Act of 1862 (also known as the Land Grant College Act), which created free agricultural colleges for ordinary citizens.

No less important—and probably more so in the eyes of future generations who believed in smaller government—the Internal Revenue Act of 1861 established a federal income tax for the first time in US history. The immediate reason was obvious: the need to redeem war bonds. By the end of the war, prosperous families—representing about one tenth of the Union's population, mostly in the Northeast—were making modest payments to the federal treasury. The principle that the rich and nearly-rich should pay more for the nation's needs was itself a step forward. Assorted tariffs and banking regulations also brought in funds to support the war. Lincoln overcame local resistance by threatening to shut down any bank that would not pay a 10% tax on state bank notes, that is, money issued locally. Now there would be *only* a national currency and a Bureau of Internal Revenue—what the Republicans had wanted all along, and Democrats had resisted—to collect tax revenues.

The changes also included one that would especially haunt democracy in the future. New regulations granted corporations legal "personhood," chartered by the federal government rather than by state governments, as in the past. Now large companies had inherent rights, including limited liability from debts and lawsuits against them. The federal government desperately needed the money gained indirectly through stimulating investments, like the giveaway of millions of Western acres to a handful of railroad corporations—who would prove to be brutal, corrupt economic tyrants. The measure indeed spurred investment, ultimately at the cost of an emerging financial aristocracy not so different from the haughty, soon-to-be banished Southern plantocracy.

The political contrast between Lincoln and Jefferson Davis, who had served as Secretary of War in a previous federal administration—far higher than any previous office held by the new Republican president—swiftly intensified. Lincoln had vast potential resources at his command. Davis depended upon King Cotton, which was vitally important to the world economy, to

JEFFERSON DAVIS

win over European allies, either by threatening European industries with boycott or with the promise of cotton smuggled out from Southern ports. Neither strategy succeeded. Surplus cotton actually glutted the wartime market, thanks in part to newer cotton-growing in distant parts of the world, while evading Northern blockades was only minimally successful. Besides, Jefferson Davis lacked the power to fully command Southern finances or even state governments for the war effort. Lincoln played this to his advantage.

THERE WILL BE BLOOD

Like his cabinet and his generals and like their counterparts in the Confederacy, Lincoln expected a short war. Current treasuries were lean, and most of the volunteers happened to be farmers, young men with families who could not afford to be away from home for long. Most Americans expected some final outcome by Christmas 1865. Lincoln planned an "Anaconda" offense to choke off Southern ports and the Mississippi River, while invading Virginia from the North, thus squeezing the South into early submission. Confederate leaders, for their part, planned to restrain Union troops, demoralizing the North into conceding Southern independence.

The Battle of Bull Run, fought near the town of Manassas, Virginia, in July, 1861, ended Lincoln's optimism. When Union lines broke, loyal troops along with journalists and curiosity-seekers fled back to nearby Washington, D.C., and the South experienced a short-lived sense of triumph. The quick victory at Bull Run even prompted some Confederate soldiers to head home, believing the war had already been won. From Lincoln's standpoint, the most dangerous consequence of Bull Run was the Democrats' craving for peace, an impulse that found its champion in a most unlikely figure. Installing young George B. McClellan, former director of the Illinois Central Railroad, as Supreme Commander of the Union Army, soon struck Lincoln as an error, but he felt that he had no choice and hoped for an improvement.

GENERAL
GEORGE McCLELLAN

McClellan himself, his optimistic expectations of a short and triumphant campaign dashed, continued drilling troops as he hesitated to engage in battle, making every excuse to continue with preparations for some uncertain future. In a short three years, he would run against Lincoln in his reelection campaign.

The next major engagement of North and South raised a different question mark for the entire war. Landing from boats into South Carolina, the Union army met not the slave owners, who had fled, but slaves who liberated themselves across the Sea Islands, broke into mansions, sang, prayed, and danced, meanwhile marking off sections of fields that, they believed, rightly belonged to them. Even the information to Lincoln conveyed through the Navy had come from an escaped slave, Robert Smalls. How the Union could best take advantage of African-American self-mobilization worried Lincoln, as he hoped that Southern-leaning border states might return to the Union, and he was still promising that they could retain their property rights in slaves. For the moment, the Union armies treated slaves as "contraband," still property but now property of the Union—an uncertain improvement in status. African-Americans had become a direct factor in the war.

The Battle of Shiloh in April, 1862, in which Southern General Albert Sidney Johnston determinedly assaulted federal troops in Tennessee, near the Mississippi border, offered a more grim portent of the conflict ahead. Back and forth the two sides fought, with virtually untrained Northerners the main victims but with massive casualties on both sides—totaling 20,000 in just a few days, more than had died during the entire first year of battle.

McClellan, meanwhile, stalled the Army of the Potomac until early 1862 and then plunged his troops into disaster after disaster. At first intending to march his forces up the Virginia Peninsula toward Richmond, he was overwhelmed again and again by Southern maneuvering, with terrible losses to his troops. In a battle that September at Antietam, Maryland—the first fought on Northern territory—the Union army halted Lee's march toward Washington, but McClellan failed to press his advantage and crush Lee's forces. In the bloodiest battle of the war, both the Union and the Confederacy lost tens of thousands more men, with only a military stalemate to show for it.

Perhaps any Union president would have appointed McClellan,

a prestigious figure in Northern society at large with an outstanding peacetime military reputation. Lincoln's judgment was truly tested through the appointment of a less prestigious figure, fellow Illinoisan Ulysses S. Grant, who had previously resigned from the Army over a problem with alcohol and, during the interim, had become the unsuccessful proprietor of a general store. First working under General Henry Halleck, Grant was soon put in charge of what was then "the West"—the area from Tennessee to the Mississippi River. Grant took his cue from John Pope, a general who would briefly succeed McClellan in Virginia, but had elaborated a military doctrine in the West that was unfamiliar to gentlemanly styles of soldiering in which civilian life was subjected to as little disruption life as possible. Pope, setting a trend for Grant and others, instructed his troops to seize food and any other supplies that they needed without compensation, and, if necessary, to execute anyone who participated in guerrilla warfare against the Union.

Pope was no match for Confederate general Robert E. Lee, but this style, known in the future as "total war," swept the West. Grant and Halleck pressed the Confederate line and the cities beyond it ever harder. Succeeding at the cost of enormous casualties, and assisted by the Union takeover of New Orleans, Grant took the city of Vicksburg, Mississippi, and moved to cut the Confederacy in two. Opening Union supply lines along the Mississippi River, he orphaned Arkansas, Louisiana, and Texas, pushing them out of the picture strategically. Farther West, Confederate efforts to gain footholds all the way to California failed. But the end was not yet in sight.

Horrific bloodshed had shown both sides, and military analysts everywhere, that war had taken on new dimensions. Generations earlier, the French general and master military strategist Napoleon Bonaparte had lost tens of thousands of troops on his march into Russian winter. The American Civil War introduced train service and with that, the possibility of massive and speedy troop movements, not to mention supplies. It also introduced new and more effective weapons, although neither side figured out how guns might replace the use of swords at anything like close range. Now, thousands could murder each other with only a few days' notice, making this, as historians noted later, the first "modern" war in the terrible history of wars. Other scholars would call it the last of the old wars, a merchant and farmers' war on both sides, unlike the twentieth century's conflicts of one industrialized country against another. Both views are probably correct.

As the crisis of war intensified, Lincoln faced his own family crisis: the death of his beloved son William ("Willie") in February, 1862. Dear to Abe in his daily life and especially during moments of stress, and dearer yet to Mary Todd Lincoln—she is thought to have lost her mental balance with Willie's death, never entirely recovering again—his loss brought an almost impenetrable gloom to the White House. Very likely, it also pushed Lincoln to a greater degree of religiosity than he had ever experienced before. This was not the happy vision of heaven for the faithful, however, but a dark vision of God's unknowable, often punishing will. Some historians describe this shift in Lincoln as a return to Calvinism, the gloom of the Middle Ages, before society gained a sense of human actions as anything but temporary and unimportant details before the arrival of Judgment Day. It might be more accurate to say that Lincoln, in tending toward religion, turned to the Old Testament. He began to see another Judgment Day ahead, approaching through the oceans of blood. America had sinned greatly, and the price would be paid.

Meanwhile, Lincoln held to his basic strategy for winning the war. In February, 1862, he wrote to General Don Carlos Buell, working under Grant, that "we have the greater numbers, and the enemy has the greater facility of concentrating forces upon points of collision; we must fail unless we can find some way of making our advantage an overmatch for his." That is, the Union would triumph by challenging and overwhelming Confederate forces at the same time in different places, so that Southern efforts to strengthen its forces in one place would weaken them somewhere else. This was a refinement of earlier ideas, in the terrible sense that widespread human loss on both sides could not be avoided.

Winning took on a subtly new framework when Republicans in Congress passed the Confiscation Act. Defeat at Bull Run had prompted even some moderates to insist that action on slavery in the seceding states would strengthen war policies as well as palliate abolitionists. Lincoln hesitated to sign the bill, partly because it changed the definition of slaves from chattel property to persons "held to labor" and freed them from owners who had used them for military purposes. That definition included the very border states Lincoln had been seeking to win over. The abolitionist-minded Union general Benjamin Franklin Butler, fighting in the West, ordered that slaves freed by this process could never be enslaved again; his successor began paying wages to escapees who joined the Union lines. Meanwhile, however, the US marshal appointed by Lincoln continued to return escapees in Maryland and Virginia to their owners. A move by General John C. Frémont, the only Republican nominee for president before Lincoln, to take things a step further in Missouri—emancipating slaves outright—prompted to his removal by President Lincoln (and thousands of protest letters). Events reached a desperate level for more dramatic steps against slavery to take hold, not necessarily from the White House but more likely from the grassroots up.

BUILDING VICTORY AT HOME

Support for Lincoln and his war policies, widespread within the North during the first weeks of the armed conflict, faded rapidly. Stephen Douglas, who had urged support for the war effort, died a few months after the firing on Fort Sumter, and Democrats soon split into pro-war and anti-war factions. Even many Republicans wavered. Lincoln urgently needed the idealists to step forward, none more ideal in this respect than the abolitionists whom he had kept at a distance until that time.

Parades, popular songs, and local recruitment committees pressed for volunteers, and financial offers ($25 to $100) followed. In 1862, a congressional bill passed at Lincoln's suggestion allowed his government to absorb state militias at will, so as to make up for the paucity of volunteers. Meanwhile, the Sanitary Commission established in June, 1861, enrolled thousands of women eager to help sick and wounded troops. Mary Livermore, an influential reformer and now leader of the commission, called it the "great channel through which the patriotic benevolence of the nation flowed to the army." Women directed twelve regional offices that provided a vast range of services for Army men and their families back home, including information on the location of wounded or imprisoned men, exerting a gendered influence on the war almost unthinkable in the past. Women also worked in military hospitals and served as army nurses, at least 3,000 of them hired and many thousands more volunteers.

A swell of popular culture building on the readership of *Uncle Tom's Cabin* made a crucial difference as well. Quaker journalist James Sloan Gibbons responded to Lincoln's appeal for volunteers with a poem that was published in a New York newspaper and became a song popular with Union troops. Set to music by the great Stephen Foster, it began with the line, "We are coming Father Abraham, three hundred thousand strong." Thus Lincoln was identified with the Old Testament patriarch of the same name. Soon, people across the North knew the lyrics:

If you look all up our valleys, where the growing harvests shine,
You may see our sturdy farmer boys fast forming into line;
And children from their mothers' knees are pulling at the weeds,
And learning how to reap and sow, against their country's needs;
And a farewell group stands weeping at every cottage door,
We are coming, Father Abraham, three hundred thousand more.

You have called us and we're coming, by Richmond's bloody tide,
To lay us down for Freedom's sake, our brother's bones beside;
Or from foul treason's savage group to wrench the murd'rous blade,
And in the face of foreign foes its fragments to parade;

Six hundred thousand loyal men and true have gone before,
We are coming Father Abraham, three hundred thousand more.

Still, the effects of other patriotic music were minor, indeed almost trivial, compared to that of a single song that was destined to be the most familiar as well as the most radical example of lyrical patriotism in all of US history.

In February, 1862, a hymn written by the well-known liberal reformer Julia Ward Howe, set to a familiar religious melody, began appearing in song sheets and within weeks was heard across the nation. Her lyrics alluded to the "end days" of the Bible's Book of Revelation, when God's harsh judgment is handed out. Union troops marching into battle and the likelihood of injury or death began singing the chorus with a different lead, "John Brown's Body Lies a Moldering in the Grave/Glory, Glory Hallelujah!... His Truth is Marching On." Howe's lyrics, with no actual mention of martyr John Brown, captured the drama of the moment:

Mine eyes have seen the glory of the coming of the Lord:
He is trampling out the vintage where the grapes of wrath are stored;
He hath loosed the fateful lightning of His terrible swift sword:
His truth is marching on.

I have seen Him in the watch-fires of a hundred circling camps,
They have builded Him an altar in the evening dews and damps;
I can read His righteous sentence by the dim and flaring lamps:
His day is marching on.

I have read a fiery gospel writ in burnished rows of steel:
"As ye deal with my contemners, so with you my grace shall deal;
Let the Hero, born of woman, crush the serpent with his heel,
His truth is marching on."

He has sounded forth the trumpet that shall never call retreat;
He is sifting out the hearts of men before His judgment-seat:
Oh, be swift, my soul, to answer Him! be jubilant, my feet!

Our God is marching on.

In the beauty of the lilies Christ was born across the sea,
With a glory in His bosom that transfigures you and me:
As He died to make men holy, let us die to make men free,
While God is marching on.

In that spirit, Mary Livermore pleaded with the president at a national council of volunteers gathering in Washington to offer a word of encouragement for the great crusade ahead. Lincoln answered wearily, "I have no word of encouragement to give!" Livermore later recalled the he had the staggering gait of a sleepwalker. In his mind, the Northern public had expected victory too easily and was unprepared for the war on the scale already begun.

Writing a note to himself after Willie's death, Lincoln strove to make sense of the horror unfolding before him, and perhaps took a more decisive turn toward something resembling religious faith. If God's logic was the same as the goal of the North—simply ending the rebellion—then He would have concluded matter quickly and decisively with the defeat of Southern forces. But the Deity obviously had something different in mind, and the conflict "shall not end yet." The true reasons for this great decision could never be known to mere human beings, Lincoln realized, but he began to suspect that the abolition of slavery was as plain a goal as Julia Ward Howe had declared in "The Battle Hymn of the Republic," or even the more popular verses of "John Brown's Body." It could not be resisted.

PATRIOTIC GORE

Even more desperate after a terrible defeat of the Union Army in Fredericksburg, Virginia, during the second week of December, 1862, Lincoln rightfully feared what was a traumatic year ahead. As his cabinet members engaged in a virtual revolt of their own, he looked for a new strategy and a new way forward. The answer, already formulating in his mind, was the Emancipation Proclamation. An argument for the morality of the war, offering a purpose for the accelerating sacrifice of young lives, it remains one of the greatest, most important documents of American history.

Courtesy of the Library of Congress

The road to the proclamation had been paved, so to speak, with decisions already made in the field and scarcely less so in Congress. Moves by a few Union generals to keep former slaves free were echoed in Congress by the Confiscation Act, which barred any future property claims by slave owners who used their slaves to aid the rebellion. Wherever Confederate troops retreated in the South, individuals or small groups of slaves left plantations by their own means.

Lincoln was fretful, and Congress moved ahead of him by ordering Union generals *not* to return any slaves to their owners. Lincoln soon caught up, however, proposing legislation that abolished slavery in Washington D.C. (with compensation for former owners) and, in the sweeping Second Confiscation Act (1862), officially declared any slaves who had escaped from Confederate owners or had been freed by the Union army as no longer slaves but "forever free." The "disloyal masters," in the phrasing of the bill Lincoln presented to Congress, had been lawfully dispossessed.

The new laws did not address slaves in the loyal border states, and they did not reconcile easily with the views of certain high officials (such as McClellan) and many ordinary Union soldiers that the slaves were not ready for freedom. Unleashed, it was feared, they might be a menace. Frederick Douglass had warned that racial prejudice blinded many good men and women, and a kind of racism had long blinded Lincoln himself. But the more he met with African American activists and intellectuals, the more he saw the determination of slaves to be free and of freed slaves to fight for their freedom, the more his heart was moved.

The worst, bloodiest part of the war lay ahead, and the Emancipation Proclamation, formally issued on January 1, 1863, made a crucial difference. Lincoln's hand was unsteady from exhaustion as he grasped his pen. Not wanting to memorialize a shaky signature, he paused a moment, said a few words, and signed the document as firmly as he could. Photographers, painters, and sculptors would depict the signing of the Emancipation Proclamation as one of the great moments in national history. And so it was, not just because the wording was so bold and direct, but because the act set apart Lincoln's decision from any other. No longer would the cooperation of slave owners be asked, and no distinction would be made between loyal and disloyal ones. The measure offered no compensation of the kind that was made to slave owners in the British Caribbean.

The proclamation did not affect loyal border states, and slavery had been abolished some places in the world—only to be restored. Above all, slavery obviously continued in the South unless and until Union troops could win the war. Yet nothing so bold as the Emancipation Proclamation had ever been ventured before. Although Lincoln described the measure as necessary to win the war, he had made himself the agent of a moral claim larger than the fighting itself. In conquered parts of the South, where African-Americans had been freed or freed themselves, as well as other parts of the country, the president now emerged as a kind of supernatural figure. Frederick Douglass, who had met with him on several occasions by this time, saw more plainly that the cause of the nation and the cause of abolition had finally merged.

The global effects were also enormous. W.E.B. Du Bois later pointed out that, with the Emancipation Proclamation, the argument of

European conservatives to recognize the South as a separate country faded rapidly. Only a few months earlier, Confederate warships harbored in English ports had awaited the moment when General Lee might capture Washington. Lecture tours by Douglass, William Lloyd Garrison, and Harriet Beecher Stowe rallied idealists on both sides of the Atlantic. And so, despite the suffering caused by a paucity of cotton for their textile mills, English working people drawn to their own great labor and social movement, Chartism, were overwhelmingly positive in their response to the Proclamation. Even before workers in the American North, English factory hands saw black slaves as workers like themselves.

The International Workingmen's Association sent a statement to Lincoln from a convention attended by 6,000 in the city of Manchester, the center of the British textile trade, that said in part, "We joyfully honor you, as the President, and the Congress with you, for the many decisive steps towards practically exemplifying your belief in the words of your great founders: 'All men are created free and equal.' We assume that you cannot now stop short of a complete uprooting of slavery.... We implore you, for your honor and welfare, not to faint in your providential mission … the vast progress you have made in the short space of twenty months fills us with hope that every stain on your freedom will shortly be removed and the erasure of that foul blot upon civilization and Christianity— chattel slavery—during your Presidency, will cause the name of Abraham Lincoln to be honored and revered by posterity."

These phrases, calling upon faith in God and devotion to the finest dreams of Christianity, were drafted by Karl Marx. Lincoln himself responded that the English workingmen were themselves a great example of "sublime Christian heroism" not "surpassed in any age or in any country." And it was true. A sacrifice across the seas had played an important role in realizing America's great step forward.

PRESIDENT-ELECT LINCOLN SLIPPED INTO THE NATION'S CAPITAL *SECRETLY*, DISGUISED AS AN INVALID.

ROBERT E. LEE

JEFFERSON DAVIS OF MISSIPPI

BETWEEN LINCOLN'S ELECTION AND HIS INAUGURATION, 12 SOUTHERN STATES FORMED THE CONFEDERACY AND DECLARED *SECESSION* FROM THE UNITED STATES. JEFFERSON DAVIS WAS SWORN IN AS THEIR PRESIDENT.

THE NATION WAS ON THE BRINK OF WAR. WASHINGTON WAS AN ARMED CAMP. U.S. ARMY SHARPSHOOTERS CROUCHED ON ROOFTOPS.

LINCOLN HAD TO FACE THE NATION'S GREATEST CRISIS WITH A CABINET OF RIVALS, SELECTED AS PART OF HIS COMPROMISE NOMINATION...

BUT SOME HISTORIANS THINK LINCOLN PREFERRED TO LEAVE HIS ADVISORS FIGHTING EACH OTHER, WHILE HE ALONE DECIDED POLICY.

ABRAHAM LINCOLN IN THE WHITE HOUSE DID NOT ACT LIKE A CELEBRITY.

MR. PRESIDENT!! YOU SHOULDN'T BE BLACKING YOUR OWN BOOTS.

"WHOSE BOOTS SHOULD I BE BLACKING?"

HIS OLDEST SON ROBERT LIVED AWAY AT COLLEGE, BUT WILLIAM AND TAD WERE THE FIRST CHILDREN IN THE WHITE HOUSE. THEY RODE THEIR PONY THRU THE RECEPTION ROOMS AND WRESTLED WITH ABE ON MARY'S EXPENSIVE ORIENTAL CARPETS.

FROM HIS WHITE HOUSE OFFICE, LINCOLN COULD SEE THE REBEL FLAGS FLYING ACROSS THE POTOMAC RIVER IN VIRGINIA.

A U.S. FORT ON AN ISLAND OFF THE COAST OF SOUTH CAROLINA WAS RUNNING OUT OF SUPPLIES. LINCOLN DISPATCHED SHIPS TO BRING FOOD FROM THE NORTH.

ON APRIL 12, 1861, CONFEDERATE BATTERIES FIRED ON FORT SUMTER. THE NATION'S BLOODIEST AND MOST BITTER WAR HAD BEGUN...

LINCOLN ISSUED A CALL FOR 75,000 VOLUNTEERS FOR ENLISTMENTS OF 90 DAYS. IN THE NATION'S CAPITAL, EVERYONE BELIEVED THE WAR WOULD END QUICKLY.

NORTH
22 MILLION

— POPULATION —

SOUTH
5 MILLION WHITE
4 MILLION SLAVE

FACTORIES PRODUCING WEAPONS

TALENTED GENERALS

RAILROADS TO TRANSPORT TROOPS & SUPPLIES

FIGHTING ON THEIR HOME TERRITORY

IN JULY, 1861, UNION TROOPS ADVANCED SOUTH INTO VIRGINIA...

OFFICIALS, NEWSMEN & TOURISTS FOLLOWED THE ARMY IN CARRIAGES. THEY PACKED PICNIC LUNCHES AND CHAMPAGNE.

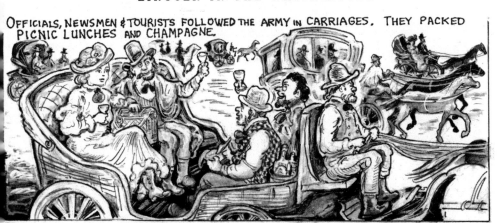

BUT AFTER A FEW HOURS UNION FORCES WERE OVERWHELMED AT A MUDDY CREEK CALLED **BULL RUN**.

SOLDIERS BROKE RANKS. EVERYONE FLED BACK TO WASHINGTON.

LINCOLN BEGAN TO STUDY BOOKS ABOUT MILITARY STRATEGY, PREPARING TO DIRECT THE WAR.

SIX GENERALS

GENERAL WINFIELD SCOTT—"OLD FUSS AND FEATHERS"—WAS **75** YEARS OLD WHEN HE COMMANDED THE UNION ARMY. HIS PLAN TO SLOWLY ENCIRCLE THE SOUTH WAS UNPOPULAR. SCOTT RESIGNED AFTER THE DISASTER AT BULL RUN.

McCLELLAN KEPT DEMANDING MORE MEN AND MONEY, DRILLING AND PARADING HIS GROWING ARMY BUT NEVER LAUNCHING AN ATTACK.

"THE PEOPLE CALL ON ME TO SAVE THE COUNTRY."

"IF GENERAL McCLELLAN HAS *NO USE* FOR THIS ARMY, I SHOULD LIKE TO BORROW IT"

NEXT UP WAS GENERAL GEORGE "LITTLE MAC" McCLELLAN. McCLELLAN HAD NOTHING BUT CONTEMPT FOR LINCOLN AND RAN AGAINST HIM IN 1864.

McCLELLAN MADE HIS REPUTATION IN THE MEXICAN WAR. HE WAS VAIN ABOUT APPEARANCE AND PIG-HEADED ABOUT STRATEGY...

After Lincoln dismissed McClellan, General Ambrose Burnside was put in charge of the Union armies. Burnside did not believe he was fit for high command and did not want the job. Burnside is remembered for his whiskers. He lost 12,000 men in a crushing defeat at Fredericksburg.

Burnside was replaced by General "Fighting Joe" Hooker. In the battle of Chancellorsville, Hooker was beaten by an army **HALF** the size of his own. 17,000 Union soldiers died on the battlefield.

General George Meade took over from Hooker. Meade was a seasoned professional soldier. Six days after taking command, Meade won a crucial Union victory at Gettysburg, Pennsylvania. But Meade was too cautious to pursue Lee into rebel territory. The war dragged on.

NOT UNTIL EARLY 1864 DID LINCOLN FIND THE GENERAL WHO WOULD WIN THE CIVIL WAR ~ ULYSSES S. "UNCONDITIONAL SURRENDER" GRANT.

GRANT LEFT THE MILITARY UNDER A CLOUD AND FAILED AT CIVILIAN LIFE, WORKING AS A CLERK IN HIS BROTHERS' LEATHER GOODS STORE.

BUT HE RE-ENLISTED IN THE CIVIL WAR AND PROVED HIMSELF FEARLESS, AGGRESSIVE, AND A CLEAR-EYED STRATEGIST.

"THE ART OF WAR IS SIMPLE ENOUGH. FIND OUT WHERE YOUR ENEMY IS. GET AT HIM AS SOON AS YOU CAN. STRIKE HIM AS HARD AS YOU CAN... AND MOVE ON."

AFTER GRANT'S VICTORIES IN THE WEST AND SOUTH, AT FORT HENRY, SHILOH, VICKSBURG AND CHATTANOOGA, LINCOLN APPOINTED HIM GENERAL-IN-CHIEF OF THE UNION ARMIES.

BUT THAT **GRANT** FELLOW IS NO BETTER THAN A COMMON *GAMBLER* AND *DRUNKARD!*

"WHATEVER BRAND GENERAL GRANT IS DRINKING, GIVE SOME TO MY OTHER OFFICERS...

GRANT SMOKED DOZENS OF CIGARS A DAY, AND CONTINUED TO DRINK HEAVILY.

CONFEDERATE FORCES WERE LED BY THE BRILLIANT, MAGNETIC MILITARY ENGINEER ROBERT E. LEE. LEE WAS A U.S. COLONEL WHO SERVED WITH DISTINCTION IN THE MEXICAN WAR. HE COMMANDED THE FORCE THAT CAPTURED RADICAL ABOLITIONIST JOHN BROWN, AFTER BROWN AND 21 SUPPORTERS RAIDED THE U.S. ARMORY AT HARPER'S FERRY.

"OBEDIENCE TO LAWFUL AUTHORITY IS THE FOUNDATION OF A MAN'S CHARACTER."

HARPER'S FERRY RAID - 1859 -

As PRESIDENT, GRANT **FAILED** TO UNITE THE COUNTRY OR ACHIEVE LINCOLN'S GOALS FOR RECONSTRUCTION.
GRANT GAVE UP HIS SOLDIER'S PENSION TO ENTER POLITICS. HE LOST HIS SAVINGS ON BAD INVESTMENTS. WHILE DYING OF CANCER GRANT WROTE **PERSONAL MEMOIRS** IN HOPES OF PROVIDING FOR HIS FAMILY. HIS BOOK WAS A HUGE SUCCESS.

" DO YOUR DUTY IN ALL THINGS. YOU CANNOT DO MORE. YOU SHOULD NEVER WISH TO DO LESS. "

ROBERT EDWARD LEE
1807-1870

LEE'S LEGENDARY **WAR HORSE** "TRAVELER"

" I HAVE NEVER ADVOCATED WAR EXCEPT AS A MEANS OF **PEACE**... "

ULYSSES SIMPSON GRANT SERVED TWO PRESIDENTIAL TERMS ~ 1869~1877

ROBERT E. LEE WAS NEVER A SLAVE~OWNER. HE WAS AN OLD-FASHIONED GENTLEMAN, LOYAL TO HIS NATIVE STATE OF VIRGINIA.
AFTER THE WAR LEE LOST HIS CITIZENSHIP AND WAS INDICTED FOR TREASON. HE SERVED AS PRESIDENT OF WASHINGTON COLLEGE IN VIRGINIA, NOW KNOWN AS WASHINGTON AND LEE UNIVERSITY.

CHAPTER FOUR

TRIUMPH AND TRAGEDY

T he causes of Northern victory and Southern defeat were many—above all the productive capacity of Northern industries and their workers to feed the Union Army and the families of men at war, while the South's desperation grew month by month. Military strategy naturally counted for much and, with Lincoln's active leadership, finally proved decisive. And yet, with all this, one unexpected element of the war loomed largest of all for US history: African-Americans' own actions.

By the end of the fighting, fully a quarter of Southern slaves had abandoned their former masters and mistresses, depriving the South of the workforce without which it could not long survive. One of the greatest historians and commentators on race in the nineteenth century, W.E. B. Du Bois, called the mass movement of individuals and families a "General Strike" of slaves. In reality, slaves did not actually go on strike so much as run away, sometimes to assist the advancing Union Army; a small fraction were actually allowed to become Union soldiers and serve in combat. On plantations that remained more or less intact until the end of the war, race relations changed radically. All in all, the slavery system was shaken if not shattered. Centuries of American history ended here, and a new chapter began.

No close observer could miss the great moral lesson of the Northern military advance, not only concerning the matter of slavery but touched on broader issues of racial identity as well. Slaves who joined the Union army and fought bravely, whose numbers increased during the last years of the war, by their actions disproved the underlying racial code of the South—along with views widely shared in the North. People of color were not genetically inferior to Americans of any other race or color, nor deficient in courage and determination on the battlefield. Thus, by implication of the Emancipation Proclamation and by demonstration in combat, denying African-American males full participation in civic life, including the vote, was shown to be a denial of deserved citizenship rights and of basic humanity.

MOVING TOWARD EMANCIPATION

Lincoln absorbed these emerging realities uneasily. By the approach of the 1862 midterm elections, increasingly disloyal Democrats had warned voters that freed blacks would run rampant, compete for their jobs, and threaten white women. Lincoln moved haltingly toward a decisive step, driven by the contradictory character of the war's stated purposes: He could no longer justify the bloodshed in the name of freedom and leave out the people held in bondage. By this time, the president had met frequently with black leaders such as Frederick Douglass and had learned a lot about the free black communities in Washington, D.C., Baltimore, and elsewhere through personal experience and information presented to him. Black and white churches in the North pressed him to move against slavery. And it finally had sunk home, after decades of pondering, that any large-scale return of colored peoples to Africa was not only impractical but unwanted. Any freed blacks who wished to return were certainly free to do so, finances permitting, but their numbers would be very small.

Nevertheless, the president recognized the political dangers as he moved toward one of the most important decisions he would ever make. Responding to Horace Greeley's newspaper editorial of August, 1962, "Prayer of Twenty Millions," calling for the immediate abolition of slavery, Lincoln still insisted that saving the Union was paramount and that he would pursue that purpose whether by freeing all slaves or by freeing only some slaves.

Then came the military imperative of September, 1862—an opportunity for McClellan to crush Lee's troops, and a blunder (as well as adept action on Lee's part) that brought the two sides together on the battlefield of Antietam, Maryland. In a horrible slaughter that left 23,000 dead or wounded, there was no clear-cut military victory for either side. Lee retreated with much of his army intact, but the Union came away with a political and moral victory, enabling Lincoln to set out his last compromise proposal to the South. Only thirty months actually remained in a war that seemed, at this point, wholly undecided one way or the either. Now, after Antietam, Lincoln declared that slave states had three months to return to the fold, and if they did, owners could keep their slaves. Slaves residing in states that were still in rebellion by the beginning of 1864, he said, would be "forever free." Challenges to the constitutionality of his proposal would be overruled by the courts, he insisted, and "those who shall have tasted actual freedom I believe can never be slaves or quasi-slaves again."

Confederate leaders were not about to return to the fold until their armies were defeated, once and for all. Lincoln's former congressional ally in opposing the Mexican invasion, Confederate vice-president Alexander Stephens, urged a peace agreement of some kind but was slapped down by those around him. Therefore, as promised on the first day of the new year, Lincoln set forth the Emancipation Proclamation. In effect, the president now sanctioned slave rebellion by suggesting that the federal government did not exclude "necessary self-defense" on the part of slaves seeking freedom. While urged to refrain from violence, they were not condemned to accept the force and physical abuse they had long endured under bondage.

European newspapers observed that Lincoln's decisive step had removed the barriers to freedom, and the effects were immediate. Later in 1864, a European labor organization summed up the consequences as follows: "From the commencement of the titanic American strife, the workingmen of Europe felt instinctively that the star-spangled banner carried the destiny of their class.... Everywhere [European workers] bore therefore patiently the hardships imposed upon them by the cotton crisis, opposed enthusiastically the pro-slavery intervention of their betters—and, from most parts of Europe, contributed their quota of blood to the good cause...." This message, given to the grandson of former president John Adams, was conveyed in a diplomatic packet to the White House. Secretary of State William Seward answered for President Lincoln, reporting his courteous and humble response to the sentiments: "They are accepted by him with a sincere and anxious desire that he may be able to prove himself not unworthy of the confidence which has been recently extended to him by ... so many friends of humanity and progress throughout the world."

This late in the day, despite the effectiveness of the Northern blockade across Southern ports and despite easy commercial access to cotton from sources other than the American South, European leaders might yet have extended the diplomatic recognition that the Confederacy so badly wanted. But The Emancipation Proclamation tipped the balance on moral grounds. The South stood isolated in the world community.

The Proclamation did not in itself end slavery. Slaves in border states loyal to the Union remained in bondage—at least for the moment. Elsewhere in the South, in places where the Union Army was not on hand to force masters to give up their slaves, the institution continued. With Lincoln's words, however, a turn of the wheel of human fate had taken place, and no one knew it better than free black populations able to celebrate Jubilee Day as promised in the Bible. Lincoln had secured his place in history for all time.

He did so in his own words, on this matter and others, largely through letters to the public. By 1863, he was giving few public addresses. Instead, he sent personal correspondences intended to serve as messages to all Americans and the world. The Loyal Publication Society printed them in tens or hundreds of thousands of copies, and they were enormously popular, widely discussed and debated. This was Lincoln's largest entry into something like the modern media, and he performed brilliantly.

THE GREAT EXCEPTION: NATIVE AMERICANS

Sadly, the contrast with federal Indian policy could not have been greater, and only few Native Americans could find any reason to celebrate Lincoln. The construction of the Transcontinental Railroad and passage of the Homestead Act had opened up the West to the ravaging of Indian lands and resources, frequently accompanied by the removal or outright slaughter of native populations, women and children included. Many tribes faced the prospect of deprivation and starvation.

The worst offenders, or at least the best-organized offenders, could often be found in the federal Indian Office, forerunner to the modern Bureau of Indian Affairs. Lincoln inherited this notoriously corrupt agency, well known for officials stealing food and other supplies while assisting in the blatant violation of treaties. Faced with the crises of civil war, Lincoln did not think it was possible, or perhaps necessary, to address all the problems with the bureau's policies or personnel. He promised to look into matters further.

The forced removal of native tribes, a continuation of longstanding federal policy, added greatly to suffering in America. In general, Lincoln exhibited toward Indians none of the understanding and little of the compassion that he expressed toward African-Americans. Nor did he have anything like the personal contact with Native American leaders that he experienced with Frederick Douglass and others representing African-American interests. The siding of several tribes with the Confederacy worsened prospects further. Kit Carson's 1863 campaign in Arizona—the forced march of 8,000 Navajos hundreds of miles into New Mexico, where a quarter of them perished and the rest remained prisoners until 1868—was one the most brutal federal responses to supposed "disloyalty."

On the other hand, Lincoln did not share the plain racial hatred or genocidal impulse toward Indians exhibited by Andrew Jackson. Lincoln's feelings could be measured in his response to the 1862 Dakota War in Minnesota, where settlers and tribes fought for months. In reviewing legal documents and sparing all but 38 of the 303 captured Indians from the hangman's noose, he demonstrated a measure of compassion for native people.

Also in 1862, President Lincoln responded to an appeal from the Principal Chief of the Cherokee Nation, John Ross, by promising a careful investigation of treaty law regarding the tribe and whether the US, in violating Indian rights, had abrogated existing treaties. He added that any Cherokees remaining loyal to the Union would "receive all the protection which can be given them consistently with the duty of the government to the whole country," and promised to protect them from any Confederate invasion. The following year, in a symbol of the sovereignty he affirmed to the Pueblo tribe—which had remained loyal to the Union—he ordered a delivery of silver-headed, ebony canes.

In his final two annual messages to Congress, in 1863 and 1864, Lincoln fretted aloud about the reforms needed in Indian policy. Yet he offered no solutions to the unfairness of the system that confined Native Americans to reservations while forcing them to negotiate away their lands piece by piece.

Nothing was so shocking as the Sand Creek Massacre in 1864, when a force of white volunteers and others under Army command in the Colorado Territory went on a sadistic rampage. Not satisfied to slaughter a whole village of Cheyenne and Arapaho while braves were away, drunken soldiers violated corpses in large numbers and, in the days that followed, displayed scalps of children and unborn fetuses as battle trophies. A federal inquiry promised better treatment through removal to another, less desirable territory—an agreement abrogated just two years later. In Lincoln's defense, he seemed hardly in control of these events from Washington, far across the country.

LINCOLN AS COMMANDER IN CHIEF

In the first years of the Civil War, Lincoln had felt hopelessly pinned down by McClellan's unwillingness to take on the enemy. Greatly pleased by Grant's advance from the West, he remained uncertain whether these victories would come in time to tilt the balance of fighting. As the 1864 election grew closer, Northern public opinion seemed to grow even wearier. Worse, draft riots by mostly Irish-Americans in New York City signaled a downright unwillingness to continue. Lincoln had the unrest put down by force, overruling state and local officials and bending the Constitution to his will.

On a previous occasion, ordering the suppression of publication and speech, Lincoln had asked, "Must I shoot a simple-minded soldier who deserts, while I must not touch a hair of a wily agitator who induces him to desert?" It was a question that hung in the air, either as an exception to constitutional rights or an invalidation of them. Meanwhile, he had to prove that victory could be won on the battlefield.

Lincoln finally dismissed General McClellan—whom he would face in the 1864 election—and appointed Ambrose Burnside as head of the Army of the Potomac. The president's chief military aim, to pursue and shatter Lee's army, thereby opening the way to conquer Richmond, led Burnside to a miscalculation. Thousands more Union soldiers were lost at Fredericksburg. Another near-debacle followed at Chancellorsville, although Lee's victory there cost him a quarter of his remaining troops, including the legendary General "Stonewall"

GENERAL
AMBROSE BURNSIDE

Jackson. Hearing the reports of Union casualties, Lincoln cried aloud, "My God, my God! What will the country say?"

Lee took a desperate course, crossing into federal territory. There, in early July, 1863, he struck Union cavalry near Gettysburg, Pennsylvania, with all his might. Union general George Meade, calling upon reserves available from everywhere, returned the fight. On the final day of the historic three-day confrontation, a desperate Southern assault on Union lines came to be known, for its commander, as "Pickett's Charge"— and resulted in the slaughter of thousands of Confederates soldiers charging into Union guns. A decisive thrust by Union forces against the disheartened Confederates might have made continuation of the war impossible for the South. But General Lee, sly as ever, escaped into Virginia with the remnant of his forces.

Lincoln, studying the big picture, sometimes seemed unaware that race had risen to the forefront in the prosecution of the war itself. General Grant, for example, not only shocked the South with his style of total warfare, depriving the residents of Vicksburg of food and water until they surrendered, but he also sent African-American infantrymen under Nathaniel Banks into battle at Port Hudson, Louisiana. The Union siege was turned back until Grant had taken Vicksburg, but the Confederates finally surrendered the port. Now the western section of the Confederacy was truly cut off, ending any hope of shipping cotton down the Mississippi River. Grant and William Tecumseh Sherman together directed Union troops successfully against Chattanooga, Tennessee, in November, 1863, leaving Atlanta, Georgia, nearly unprotected.

The all-black 54th Massachusetts Regiment joined the Union attack near Charleston in July, 1863, but a bungled strategy resulted in wholesale death. As in Port Hudson, the brave showing of black infantrymen dispelled any expectations of the contrary, North or South. Strategically, if not for hopes that the coming election would unseat Lincoln, the South was effectively defeated because it could no longer sustain its military force or its civilian population much longer.

Perhaps for that reason alone, a war that had begun in a kind of gentlemanly manner with mutual expectations of a quick ending took on a more savage character. Faced with the prospect of free African-Americans, Confederate soldiers and their commanders came to regard Union forces as their mortal enemies, to be slaughtered wherever possible instead of merely defeated or captured. Murdering Union soldiers who sought surrender, Southern troops sometimes practiced what they regarded as the ultimate violation of corpses, throwing whites in with blacks. Guerrilla fighting moved in where organized opposition to Northern troops dissolved. From Virginia to Kansas, Confederate freebooters carried out mass executions of Union-sympathizing civilian families, decapitations, and other outrages, while the much-feared terror by black populations against whites remained a myth of white supremacists. The major action continued on the battlefield.

Not far from the fighting, Southern troops attended religious revivals that reached a peak during 1863-64, pumping up their courage and resolve to preserve the White Kingdom against the race-mixing outsiders. Inevitably, at least in their minds, a God on the side of white supremacy would surely save the Confederacy. No Christian charity was to be extended to the enemy.

And so the bloodshed continued. At the end of November, 1864, outside Franklin, Tennessee, Southern General John Bell Hood took a brave stand, hoping to vanquish Yankee invaders with a sudden march on their entrenched guns. Each side had about 20,000 soldiers amassed on the front lines; beyond them, the Union had another 60,000 in reserve. As a result, no less than six Confederate generals died in the battle; entire Southern regiments were wiped out. Observers called it a "Holocaust," predicting the horrors in Europe many generations in the future.

Grant pushed on, driving Confederates out of the Appalachian Mountains. Union victories at Missionary Ridge and Lookout Mountain prompted Lincoln to bring Grant to the East and promote him to general-in-chief of the entire Union Army, putting him alongside the president as the key strategist for the final push. General Lee sought to strike before Grant could muster his forces. Despite being heavily outnumbered in the Chancellorsville campaign, Lee and his forces left 17,000 Union troops dead, wounded, or missing. Grant, rather than retreat, struck back hard at the cost of 18,000 casualties at Spotsylvania and thousands more at Cold Harbor.

Pushing ahead toward Richmond, sometimes taking disastrous chances, Grant sought to exhaust Confederate resources, human and otherwise, in victory or defeat. He set his sights on Richmond and everything along the way. Around Petersburg, the strategic gate to the Confederate capital, Grant decided on siege warfare. The stranglehold lasted ten months, well into 1865. As Lincoln listened closely for reports, both sides dug in. Union assaults failed to break through Confederate lines, but Lee could no longer risk a counterattack.

When Grant had been moved East, Lincoln turned over the Western command to William Tecumseh Sherman. Lincoln trusted General Sherman in the way he trusted Grant—as a bold, unrestrained fighter. Sherman was also wily, refusing to expose his entire force to danger, instead poking and prodding the Confederates as he moved steadily east. Approaching Atlanta, Sherman may have turned the political tide of the 1864 elections one way or the other. His victory on the battlefield would help secure Lincoln's reelection, but the risk was great.

GENERAL WILLIAM
TECUMSEH SHERMA[N]

Sherman's next step was strategic genius, perhaps the most important tactical decision of the war. He determined to "ruin Georgia," setting fires in Atlanta instead of invading it and turning instead to the undefended countryside. In his infamous March to the Sea, Sherman's forces looted plantations, freeing slaves in the process, pulled out railroad ties (heated and bent around trees, they became "Sherman's Neckties"), and destroyed cities and towns all along the way. It was now a total war against the slave system. Sherman himself recalled later that his troops broke out into song, "John Brown's Body," in something approaching perfect rhythm and pitch, as if they had been born to sing those lines.

Had Lincoln sought to restrain the burning and destruction, he might not have succeeded. When Sherman marched into South Carolina, his troops continued their own way, pursuing the retreating Confederate troops, not halting public food riots against Southern authorities, and encouraging the now-widespread desertion of Confederate soldiers from their own army. As Lincoln had intuited, poor Southern whites—faced with near-starvation of themselves and their families back home, watching while the rich continued to enjoy a different lifestyle, even in these conditions—had finally lost their will to fight. Confederate resistance began to crumble, in many places, at the approach of battle.

THE HOMEFRONT
AND THE DECISIVE ELECTION

The greatest contradiction in Lincoln's presidency was undoubtedly the acceleration of the division between rich and poor in many loyal parts of the Union. Not only did the need to borrow money to pay for the war compel the government to sell bonds that would bring enormous profits to bondholders, but war profiteering boomed: shoddy shoes were sold the Army, spoiled beef sickened thousands of soldiers (at a fine profit to vendors), and thin blankets went to the field instead of the thick ones paid for by taxes.

It was in part poverty and in part an unfair draft, in which the wealthy could buy their way out of service by hiring replacements, that prompted mainly Irish crowds in New York City to outright violence in July, 1863. In addition to rioting, burning draft offices, and attacking the residences of the city's wealthy elite, they perpetrated beatings, murder, and arson upon African Americans. Asked by New York governor Horatio Seymour to halt the riots by rescinding the draft, Lincoln wrote that he could not do so because "time is too important," adding "we are contending with an enemy, who ... drives every able-bodied man he can reach into his ranks.... This produces an army which will soon turn upon our now victorious soldiers, already in the field, if they shall not be sustained by recruits as they should be."

Meanwhile, the advance of industrialization often prompted a deepening sense of class division along with all the progress it brought across the North, the emerging Plain States, and the Far West. Mechanized farm implements, for example, became essential to a family whose husband and father was away at war; the McCormick Reaper allowed sturdy farm wives, perhaps with some hired help or the cooperation of neighbors, to manage at harvest time. Many farm families without the funds for such equipment simply failed. And the new equipment required iron, which spurred the mining industry. Demand for a host of minerals, along with the discovery of gold, fueled a mining boom in the West. Expansion of railroad lines alone created a higher demand for goods than the output of whole nations in Europe. Although new fortunes were created overnight, existing fortunes among bankers, railroad bondholders, and assorted financiers gained most from the burgeoning economy.

Lincoln's praises of "free labor" sounded rather hollow for workingmen and working women who tried to create the first labor unions in their trades, or to revive union efforts that had bloomed earlier in a few East Coast. Even highly skilled and well-organized German immigrants in trades as familiar to them as brewing beer faced a vicious response from employers. Ordinary American working people with no union experience were generally beaten down—sometimes literally by police, more often replaced by non-union workers. Men and women known to be union organizers were placed on blacklists, making it impossible for them to find in work in the same industry anywhere. For dwellers of ever-expanding city slums, a short walk across town could take them to mansions with fine furnishings, servants, and expensively dressed men, women, and children who regarded working people as little better than slaves—that is, "wage slaves."

ELECTION POLITICS AND RACE

Lincoln quashed a "palace revolution," sought by Salmon Chase, to replace the current cabinet with another, more radical one. Likewise, he fended off radical opposition to his own renomination for president in 1864. With Sherman's march through Georgia and the tide of war having turned, he seemed to be safely in power. But in responding to factions proposing abolitionist-minded General Frémont as the party's nominee, Lincoln made sure that both his keynote speech at the convention in Baltimore and the key plank in the Republican platform demand the end of slavery and the unconditional surrender of the Confederacy. Now, if not before, abolition became the inevitable consequence of Union victory. Lincoln's letter of acceptance contained an appeal, his first, for a Thirteenth Amendment.

Meanwhile, so-called Peace Democrats, or Copperheads, led by former Congressman Clement Vallandigham of Ohio, continued to urge an armistice with slavery preserved. Vallandigham, exiled to Canada, hinted that the new Western states and territories might secede as well, joining the South in a new national body allied against the Northeast and especially against the abolitionists. Lincoln's repressive measures in response to the threat, quashing open dissent, succeeded in some ways but cost him dearly among those who valued civil liberties.

The greater danger came from an ugly, swelling tide of racism. Another Ohio politician, Democratic Congressman Samuel S. Cox, delivered a speech on the floor of the House denouncing a pamphlet titled *Miscegenation: The Theory of the Blending of the Races, Applied to the White Man and Negro* and attributed the racist philosophy to Republican colleagues. The document was a hoax, however, written and published by an editor and reporter for the *New York World*, a Democratic publication that would do anything to stop Lincoln. Democrats promised in posters and speeches to "defeat Negro Equality" and return prosperity, along with peace.

The tide of politics and war seemed, for an extended period, to bode ill for the Republican Party facing a newly strengthened opposition. "I am going to be beaten," Lincoln had told one of his leading Army officers in 1864, "and unless some great change takes place, badly beaten." Democratic legislators controlling several states vowed that they would not accept absentee ballots, even from Union soldiers in the field. But the celebrations that broke out in cities across the North at the news of Sherman's victory in Atlanta in July, 1864, foretold the outcome of the fall elections.

STRUGGLE FOR
THE THIRTEENTH AMENDMENT

Lincoln had been asked by an Illinois congressman late in 1863 to propose an amendment to the US Constitution that would eliminate legal slavery once and for all. Focused strategically on a plan that could proceed from state by state, winning allies for the war effort along the way, Lincoln demurred. Congressmen and senators moved ahead on their own, apparently without success. A few Democrats supported the idea, while Republicans pressed the notions that each man was entitled to the fruits of his labor and that the continuation of slavery threatened the republic. After months of debate, the Thirteenth Amendment passed the Senate overwhelmingly in April, 1864—then failed in the House, with Democrats voting almost unanimously against it. Assorted measures to weaken the status of slave owners did pass, such as the repeal of the notorious Fugitive Slave Act, but none could be seen as decisive.

Radicals demanding more drastic measures also got a bill through Congress that would free the slaves and guarantee their rights in successfully reconstructed Southern states. Lincoln, placing military victory ahead of political objectives, exercised a "pocket veto," allowing the measure to die with the end of the congressional session. Radicals, including an increasing number of Republicans, looked ahead in a different way, keenly aware that the future of their party in the South depended upon black votes.

But electoral politics soon came to the fore. As Democrats moved to nominate General McClellan on a platform leaving Southern slavery intact, Lincoln despaired privately, hinting that if the Supreme Court were to declare that slaves could not be freed by presidential proclamation, he would resign rather than accept the return of slaves to bondage. Then, at the low point of Lincoln's confidence, Sherman's army swept into Atlanta. Perhaps the most impressive result in November was that nearly 80% of Union soldiers voted for Lincoln against their former commander, McClellan. Lincoln won 55% of the popular vote overall, and the opposition was soundly defeated—at least until the war ended.

Lincoln's overwhelming electoral victory and the enhanced majorities of Republicans in both houses of Congress put the Thirteenth Amendment at the forefront of the legislative agenda. In his post-election message to Congress, the president reiterated his support for the amendment, urging passage sooner rather than later.

A great lobbying campaign ensued on Capitol Hill, with many promises made to swing voters: patronage appointments at all levels, ambassadorships, and a political argument promising the consolidation of Republican strength. The House voted in favor of the amendment, 119 to 56, slightly more than the required two-thirds majority, on the last day of January, 1865. With the Senate having already given its approval, the stage was set for ratification. Three quarters of all states (Lincoln insisted at the total should be included the Confederate states) would be required for ratification, which came before the end of the year.

RECONSTRUCTION?

The approaching Union victory, meanwhile, raised an issue that many had long avoided: What would be the life of people of color in the "reconstructed" South? African-Americans could and did become Army officers, black clergy could conduct prayers in Congress, and black lawyers could bring cases before the Supreme Court. Discriminatory "black laws" had ended in nearly every Northern state. But what would happen in the South?

The president, as of early 1865, had not yet been convinced of the necessity to demand that black men be allowed to vote in the reconstructed states. For him, even this late, voting remained a state prerogative. For abolitionists, voting power was the final proof that citizenship had finally arrived.

It was the pressure of war that had first impelled the transfer of land from white to black hands. General Sherman issued an order that directed the transfer of the Sea Islands off the coast of Georgia, along with a wide swath of land in that state and South Carolina, into forty-acre plots for African American families; with the land came a mule supplied by the Army to help work it. Thus the slogan "forty acres and a mule" came into the vocabulary of Reconstruction.

PRESIDENT
ANDREW JOHNSON

Lincoln declined to advance or overrule Sherman's mandate and agreed with Congress to establish what would become the Freedman's Bureau. Black and white war refugees—but mainly former slaves—would receive assistance from the new federal agency. The Bureau lasted only a few years but, in that time, established schools, courts, and other means of uplift and redress. After Lincoln's death, President Andrew Johnson returned all confiscated land to former white owners, breaking the promise of "forty acres and a mule."

Lincoln's failure on this score may have been rooted in his past as a lawyer for property holders and corporations. It may also have reflected the drastic changes taking place in American society, with economic power concentrated in ever-fewer hands. But it was surely his belief as well that the sin of slavery and the hope of redemption lay in the whole nation and not only in the South. Abolitionists insisted that equality for all races must come before forgiveness, while Lincoln himself spoke more and more movingly of the judgments of God. Frederick Douglass shrewdly described Lincoln's Second Inaugural address, on March 4, 1865, as a sermon, not a policy statement. Perhaps the president was too physically and psychologically worn to do more.

But there was more in this address, considered a masterpiece of political oratory, which he delivered a mere six weeks before his assassination and was, in that way, a sort of last testament. The president looked weak on the day of his inauguration, not broken physically but bone-tired and shaken by all that had transpired in the last four years. The audience stood quietly and, in the era before sound amplification, listened hard for every word. Lincoln began modestly, not only about the occasion but about the coming of the war that men on both sides had been unable to avert. The Union "might not be perfect," he admitted, "but it was clearly on the side of the angels."

Both sides, he reminded listeners, "read the same Bible, and pray to the same God; and each invokes His aid against the other." It was strange, he went on "that any men should dare to ask a just God's assistance in wringing their bread from the sweat of other men's faces." As an aside he quoted the New Testament phase, "let us judge not, that we not be judged," followed by words from the Old Testament: "Woe to that man by whom the offense cometh!" Then he went straight to the point:

If we suppose that American Slavery is one of those offences which, in the providence of God, must needs come, but which having continued through His appointed time, He now wills to remove, and that He gives to both North and South, this terrible war as the woe due to those by whom the offence came, shall we discern therein any departure from those divine attributes which the believers in a Living God always ascribe to Him? Fondly do we hope—fervently do we pray—that this mighty scourge of war may speedily pass away. Yet, if God wills that it continue, until all the wealthy piled by the bondsman's two hundred and fifty years of unrequited toil shall be sunk, and until every drop of blood drawn with the lash shall be paid by another drawn with the sword, as was said three thousand years ago, so it must be said, "the judgments of the Lord, are true and righteous altogether."

Most readers remember the catch phrase, "with malice toward none; with charity for all," but likely miss the deeper spiritual implications of the address. Lincoln took an extraordinary step. American theologians and many others before and after Lincoln's time have insisted that the United States is a favorite of the Deity, deemed "exceptional" because of a task to lead the world. Perhaps America would lead or guide the world beginning with the "American Century," as *Time* magazine designated the twentieth, or perhaps going forward into the infinite future, as a virtuous and benign power. Politicians, orators, writers, and historians—with few exceptions until the 1960s—insisted that if slavery were so profoundly wrong, it was certain to have ended at some time, perhaps peacefully, anyway. Abolitionists, the troublesome minority, were not treated kindly by these writers.

The passages in the Bible nearest to Lincoln's words, however, may be found in Old Testament condemnations of collective moral failure by the prophet Isaiah. Isaiah insisted that the children of Israel had been condemned to suffer by their abandonment of righteousness and their own sin. In Lincoln's Address, the United States is not without sin. Slavery had been an intimate part of American life since colonial times and the founding of the nation, whose constitution accepted slavery as a rightful expression of property.

Lincoln's critics, in the press and elsewhere, chastised him for talking "theology" when the occasion called for civics. For this he had a ready answer, actually a letter he wrote to Republican leader Thurlow Weed: "Men are not flattered by being shown that there has been a difference in purpose between the Almighty and them.... I thought it needed to be told."

On other occasions, Lincoln had spoken of a God whose purpose could not be easily or precisely understood. The war, and doubtless the actions of African-Americans from the plantation to the battlefield to the homefront of freed blacks in the North, likely convinced him to take a stronger stand on this occasion. The savagery of Southern troops toward African Americans fighting for freedom was likely another motivation. The murderers of black humanity were the hounds of hell, and perhaps, though Lincoln did not say it, the temptation of slavery as an economic tool and a social organizing concept had been the Serpent in the Garden, the New World garden of hope for humanity to be redeemed from its past sins.

One month later, on April 4, Lincoln toured the conquered Confederate capital of Richmond, days behind Union troops led by an all-black regiment from Massachusetts. As correspondents recalled, crowds of blacks seeking a glimpse of Lincoln shouted, "GLORY GLORY GLORY!" The "surging mass of men, women and children, black, white and yellow, running, shouting dancing, swinging their caps, bonnets and handkerchiefs," was a sight that had been unthinkable only a short time earlier. A few white women waved from the windows of their houses; others looked disgusted at the sight of him. Lincoln himself said, "Yesterday morning the majority of the thousands who crowded the streets and hindered our advance were slaves. Now they were free." And as a former slave kneeled before him, the president famously told him, "You must kneel to God only, and thank Him for the liberty you will enjoy hereafter." Leaving Richmond, he asked the Union army band to play the Marsellaise, in honor of a visiting French guest, and then to play Dixie, for "it was good to show the rebels that, with us in power, they will be free to hear it again."

THE WAR ENDS, MARTYRDOM FOLLOWS

The collapse of Southern resistance, so long delayed, came despite a series of tactical victories by outnumbered Confederate troops under the wily Lee, who was as brilliant in defensive maneuvers as in taking the offensive. Retreating ever further, the general agreed with an astounding proposal of Confederate leaders: to draft slaves for military use, promising, but not in writing, to free them for their sacrifice. Two black regiments may have been organized (the evidence is disputed), but it was too late.

Confederate president Jefferson Davis sent his vice-president, Alexander Stephens, to Hampton Roads, Virginia, to negotiate a peace. The offer was met with Lincoln's offer of gradual emancipation, including financial compensation for slave owners. (This model had served the British in parts of the Caribbean, with lasting bitterness among former slaves who felt that *their* labor and lives had been stolen for centuries and that the compensation was delivered to the wrong party.) Lincoln also insisted on total surrender of the South, while Davis had directed Stephens to demand that the South retain its political independence. The negotiations failed.

If the defeat of Pickett's Charge in the Battle of Gettysburg would go down in history as the "Waterloo of the Confederacy," as large in the scope of military sagas as Napoleon's crushing defeat in 1815, Grant's assault on Petersburg was truly the beginning of the end for Lee and the Confederacy. Lincoln had met Grant and Sherman on board a ship, the *River Queen*, and made clear that Lee had to be trapped this time, without hope of escape. Grant and Sherman told him that blood would flow like water, to which the president responded, "Can't you spare more effusions of blood?" To no avail.

Grant bore down on Lee at Petersburg with a force of 100,000 soldiers, to Lee's 50,000. Lincoln watched the fires flashing from the River Queen, as Confederate lines collapsed and Lee resolved to escape, one last time, west along the Appomattox River.

Lincoln had offered compromise early on and later sought victory at all costs. Now he moved to close the deal. As the president himself was entering Richmond, Union forces led by General Philip Sheridan overtook the back side of Lee's retreating army. More than a quarter of all Lee's remaining troops, exhausted and hungry, surrendered. Lee and the last of his men pushed ahead in hopes of recovering supplies at the Appomattox railroad station. Sheridan and his cavalry got there first, and Lee had no choice but to give up.

Lincoln's tour of Richmond came just five days before Lee surrendered to Grant at Appomattox Court House on April 9, 1865. At Lincoln's suggestion, the broken Southern troops were given three days' provisions and sent home to rebuild their lives. Granted parole, they could not be legally prosecuted, no matter what crimes they had perpetrated upon civilians. Jefferson Davis fled south, hoping to launch a new campaign from Texas, but was soon captured. Small bands of Southerners continued fighting in a desultory manner, mostly attacks upon civilians and their property, in Missouri and elsewhere. So did bands of Indians in the West—Cherokee, Choctaw, Creek, Seminole, and Osage—heeding promises of land made by Confederate leaders and finding no allies in the Union. The resistance in all cases remained isolated; the war was over in any meaningful sense.

WHAT WAS LEFT BEHIND?

"Here was a land," wrote W.E.B. Du Bois about the South of 1865, of "poignant beauty, streaked with hate and blood and shame, where God was worshipped wildly, where human beings were bought and sold, and where even in the twentieth century men are burned alive.... Here were people who knew they knew one thing above all others ... that a Negro would not work without compulsion, and that slavery was his natural condition." Even as Southern states, led by Louisiana, reentered the Union, they enacted Black Codes to punish and exploit the freed slaves in a hundred ways. The Union victory was already diminished.

Ironically, the last Confederate troops to surrender, on May 26, 1865, did so in Indian Territory (now Oklahoma), leaving behind guerrilla fighters from tribes seeking a more equitable treatment from the government. On top of the grievous losses suffered in this and other territories, not to mention the myriad human rights violations, the continuing conflict was a sad token of unending racial inequality.

THE NATION'S GREATEST MARTYR

Lincoln's final days were happy, especially the last one on April 14, 1865. "And well I may feel so," he told Mary Todd Lincoln, "for I consider this day, the war has come to a close. We must both be more cheerful in the future." Mary recalled that he was "cheerful—almost joyous" that day. When his presidency was over, the couple planned to visit Europe and California, and then return home to Illinois. They were not yet sixty years old. There was good reason to think they might have many calm and pleasant times ahead.

At Richmond, Lincoln had told Admiral David Porter, "Thank God I have lived to see this. It seems to me that I have been dreaming a horrid dream for four years, and now the nightmare is gone." Sadly, the nightmare had not ended, and Lincoln would not live to enjoy the days of jubilation. He had long anticipated that he might not survive the war, which weighed on him heavily as he made decisions that cost many thousands more lives.

On the night of April 14 At Ford's Theater in Washington, D.C., Lincoln was shot in the head at close range. He died the next day.

The assassin, a Southern sympathizer named John Wilkes Booth, had stood in the crowd listening to Lincoln's Second Inaugural Address the previous month, silently swearing revenge. Booth had written his own theological interpretation, reflecting the view of most Southerners. "This country was formed for the white, not the black man," he believed, and slavery was among the "greatest blessings" afforded by God to the chosen nation. Lincoln, in Booth's view, had defied the most basic theology of the South, from the arrival of the first slaves in Virginia to the end of the Civil War. Lincoln had died, of course, to undo that history and save the Union.

The national outpouring of grief—except in most of the white South—was unprecedented. Indeed it was the beginning of a sustained anguish for all those who had died in the war and for the survivors who had been damaged, mentally and physically, perhaps for the rest of their lives. The largest crowd ever to gather at the White House, up to 25,000 people, came to pay their respects. Wounded soldiers, women, and children filed past the coffin, crying unashamedly. A throng of 60,000 stood outside, waiting to do the same. Public viewing continued until the start of a 1700-mile funeral train to Springfield, with numerous dignitaries on board.

As Lincoln's remains passed from city to city, crowds of every social class and color gathered along the tracks to pay tribute. Thousands wrote memorial poetry, so many that newspapers warned readers that only a small fraction of those submitted could be published. The crowd in New York City was especially large, but Chicago was the last and biggest gathering for the dead leader—up to 100,000 mourners in all. Days later, some 75,000 met the train in Springfield itself for the funeral itself. Meanwhile, in a footnote to history, John Wilkes Booth had been killed in Virginia, shot by pursuers after being trapped in a burning burn.

The most famous of poems to survive into the next century and beyond was surely Walt Whitman's elegy, beginning with the words, "Oh Captain, My Captain!" Whitman assumed a more philosophical tone in another of his Lincoln series, "When Lilacs Last in the Dooryard Bloom'd." In it he wrote, "A star in the sky brings back the memory of the fallen leader, but also does the sound of birds and flowers?" The "shy and hidden bird" mourns the passing of the coffin bearing Lincoln, and Whitman asks "How shall I warble myself to the dead one there I loved?" He gives his answer to the beautiful winged creature:

> Sing on, there in the swamp!
> O singer bashful and tender! I hear your notes—I hear your call;
> I hear—I come presently—I understand you;
> But the moment I linger—for the lustrous star has detain'd me.
> The star, my departing comrade, holds and detains me

Whitman had seen the peace that follows the slaughter, and consoled himself that Lincoln was also at peace. But he could not move on without remembering everything that Lincoln, truly Father Abraham, has meant to him and the nation.

FATHER ABRAHAM

WHEN MARY TODD LINCOLN MOVED INTO THE WHITE HOUSE SHE FOUND IT SHABBY AND NEGLECTED, WITH PEELING WALLPAPER, TATTERED DRAPES, MOLD AND MICE IN THE STORE ROOMS...

MARY SET TO WORK ORDERING REPAIRS, SUPERVISING THE NECESSARY CARPENTRY, PLASTERING AND PAINTING.

MARY REPLACED BROKEN CHAIRS AND TORN CURTAINS. BUT WASHINGTON SOCIETY SAW HER EFFORTS AS PROOF THEIR NEW FIRST LADY WAS A CRUDE *SHOW OFF,* SQUANDERING PUBLIC FUNDS IN WARTIME.

THEY *SAY* THE NEW DINING SET WAS CUSTOM BUILT BY THE MOST EXPENSIVE SHOWROOM IN NEW YORK!

SHE'S TEN YEARS *TOO OLD* AND TEN POUNDS *TOO FAT* FOR THOSE LOW CUT GOWNS WITH ALL THE FLOWERS!

THE WORST OF IT IS—TWO OF HER VERY OWN COUSINS SERVE IN THE *REBEL ARMY!*

© SHARON RUDAHL 2013

130

MARY INVITED 500 SELECT GUESTS TO A PARTY FEBRUARY 2, 1862, TO PRESENT THE RESTORED WHITE HOUSE... GENERALS IN DRESS UNIFORMS, DIPLOMATS, SUPREME COURT JUSTICES, FASHIONABLE WIVES AND DAUGHTERS ARRIVED AT 9:00 P.M.

A FEW DAYS BEFORE THE GALA, TAD HAD BEGUN COMPLAINING OF *STOMACH ACHE.* HE AND WILLIE WERE BOTH FEVERISH BY PARTY TIME...

ONLY A TOUCH OF BILIOUS FEVER...

THE BOYS ARE IN *NO DANGER.* GO BACK TO YOUR GUESTS.

THE WHITE HOUSE STAFF WORE NEW BERRY RED UNIFORMS TO MATCH THE NEW CHINA.

YOUR WIFE HAS ACCOMPLISHED *WONDERS!*

WHAT A FEATHER IN YOUR CAP, MRS. LINCOLN —

A WHITE HOUSE WE CAN ALL FEEL **PROUD** OF AGAIN...

THE U.S. MARINE BAND PLAYED A NEW SONG WRITTEN FOR THE OCCASION...

AND NOW, LADIES & GENTLEMEN, IT IS MY HONOR TO PRESENT ~ THE MARY LINCOLN POLKA *!!*

132

All public receptions at the White House were cancelled.

Through this darkest of all Lincoln's dark spells, he continued to work eighteen hour days.

Willie had been Lincoln's favorite. When he found a spare moment, Lincoln locked himself in his office to weep alone.

IN THE CIVIL WAR PERIOD, SPIRITUALISM WAS BECOMING POPULAR. MEDIUMS CLAIMED THEY COULD CONTACT THE **AFTERWORLD**. MARY LINCOLN TRIED TO CONJURE UP HER DEAD SONS...

THE LINCOLNS WERE NOT **ALONE** IN THEIR GRIEF. ACROSS THE UNITED STATES, MANY THOUSANDS OF FAMILIES MOURNED DEAD SONS, BROTHERS, HUSBANDS...

THE **CIVIL WAR** DRAGGED ON WITHOUT CONVINCING UNION VICTORIES. DISCONTENT BREWED.

IT'S **HIGH TIME** LINCOLN FREED THE SLAVES!!

ABOLITION NOW

JOHN BROWN LIVES

PEACE NOW

STATES RIGHTS

NO DRAFT

FOR ALL ARE EQUAL

DIXIE

IT'S **HIGH TIME** WE MADE **PEACE** WITH OUR SOUTHERN BROTHERS!!!

ONE CLEAR VOICE FOR ABOLISHING SLAVERY WAS THE ORATOR AND JOURNALIST **FREDERICK DOUGLASS.** HE WAS BORN INTO SLAVERY IN 1817.

SELF-LIBERATED AND SELF-EDUCATED, DOUGLASS FOUNDED A NEWSPAPER—THE NORTH STAR. THE MOTTO ON ITS MASTHEAD WAS: "ALL RIGHTS FOR ALL."

SNAP

DOUGLASS COMPLAINED THAT THE UNION WAS FIGHTING THE REBELS WITH **ONE HAND**—

"... WHILE KEEPING THEIR **IRON BLACK HAND** CHAINED AND HELPLESS BEHIND THEM."

WHEREVER UNION ARMIES ADVANCED, ESCAPED SLAVES RUSHED TO JOIN THEM.

136

SLAVES WHO FLED THE PLANTATIONS WERE EAGER TO DEFEAT THE CONFEDERACY. ENROLLED IN BLACK REGIMENTS, THEY FOUGHT WITH IMPRESSIVE COURAGE AND DISCIPLINE. BY THE END OF THE CIVIL WAR, 180,000 AFRICAN-AMERICANS SERVED IN THE UNION ARMIES.

SLAVES COULD BE CLAIMED BY UNION FORCES AS "CONTRABAND" REBEL PROPERTY. BUT THEY MIGHT BE RETURNED TO BONDAGE AS BATTLE LINES SHIFTED.

ON SEPTEMBER 22, 1862, LINCOLN READ THE FINAL WORDING OF HIS EMANCIPATION PROCLAMATION TO HIS CABINET. HIS CAREFUL LAWYER'S JUSTIFICATION WAS MILITARY NECESSITY.

"...ESSENTIAL TO THE PRESERVATION OF THE UNION..."

"...ON JANUARY 1, 1863, ALL PERSONS HELD AS SLAVES IN REBEL TERRITORY WOULD BE THEN, THENCE FORWARD AND *FOREVER FREE.*"

NEW YEAR'S EVE, 1862~ IN THE NORTH, ABOLITIONISTS CELEBRATED. CONGREGATIONS OF FREE BLACKS OFFERED UP PRAYERS OF THANKS.

"THE CAUSE OF THE SLAVES AND THE CAUSE OF THE COUNTRY HAVE BECOME *ONE.*"

TWO OF FREDERICK DOUGLASS' SONS WERE AMONG MANY NEW VOLUNTEERS FOR THE UNION ARMIES.

IN THE SOUTH, NEWS OF EMANCIPATION DID NOT REACH EVERY ISOLATED PLANTATION... BUT WHERE SLAVES *KNEW,* IF ONE HAD A TIMEPIECE, MANY GATHERED TO AWAIT THE HOUR OF FREEDOM.

GETTYSBURG, PENNSYLVANIA
NOVEMBER 19, 1863

© SHARON RUDAHL 2013

"WAR IS HELL"

GENERAL W. T. SHERMAN

WE REMEMBER THE CIVIL WAR AS A THRILLING ADVENTURE STORY, WITH HEROS IN COSTUMES, DRAMATIC BATTLES, AND A GREAT MORAL VICTORY OVER SLAVERY. BUT THE CIVIL WAR COST AT LEAST 850,000 LIVES, MORE THAN ALL OTHER U.S. WARS TOGETHER. AND IT LEFT SCARS THAT STILL DIVIDE OUR NATION...

AS COMMANDER IN CHIEF, LINCOLN AUTHORIZED HIS ARMY OFFICERS TO ARREST ANYONE WHO OBSTRUCTED THE DRAFT OR AIDED THE REBELS.

LET'S MAKE *PEACE* WITH OUR SOUTHERN BROTHERS!!

NO DRAFT

PEACE NOW

LINCOLN SUSPENDED THE RIGHT OF *HABEAS CORPUS*. THIS MEANT SUSPECTS COULD BE HELD WITH-OUT TRIAL. BY THE SUMMER OF 1863, MORE THAN 13,000 ANTI-WAR PRISONERS CROWDED NORTHERN PRISONS.

SUPREME COURT CHIEF JUSTICE TANEY DECLARED LINCOLN'S SUSPENSION OF CIVIL LIBERTIES *UNCONSTITUTIONAL*. BUT LINCOLN HELD FIRM:

"MUST I SHOOT A SIMPLE-MINDED SOLDIER BOY WHO DESERTS WHILE I MUST NOT TOUCH A HAIR OF THE WILY AGITATOR WHO URGES HIM TO DESERT?"

~LINCOLN OFTEN PARDONED DESERTERS...

IN 1862, THE CONFEDERACY PASSED THE FIRST U.S. DRAFT LAW. THE UNION DRAFT BEGAN THE NEXT YEAR. ALL ABLE-BODIED MEN AGES 20-45 WERE SUBJECT TO MILITARY CONSCRIPTION...

"... OR THE DRAFTEE MAY *HIRE* A SUBSTITUTE OR PAY $300. TO BE *EXEMPT*"!?!

THE BLOOD OF A *POOR MAN* IS AS PRECIOUS AS A RICH MAN'S!

THERE WERE DRAFT RIOTS IN SEVERAL NORTHERN CITIES. ON JULY 12, 1863, NEWSPAPERS IN NEW YORK PUBLISHED THE NAMES DRAWN IN ITS DRAFT LOTTERY. THE CITY ERUPTED. 50,000 RIOTERS FLOODED INTO THE STREETS. THEY SET FIRE TO THE DRAFT BOARD, ATTACKED THE MAYOR'S HOUSE, AND CLUBBED DOWN AFRICAN AMERICANS. THE RIOTERS WERE MOSTLY POOR IMMIGRANTS FROM IRELAND AND CENTRAL EUROPE. IN 4 DAYS OF VIOLENCE, 500 CIVILIANS WERE KILLED.

MORE THAN 500 CIVILIANS DIED IN THE RIOTS. PEACE WAS RESTORED BY UNION TROOPS RUSHED FROM GETTYSBURG TO NEW YORK.

IN FOUR UNION DRAFT CALLS, ABOUT 800,000 NAMES WERE DRAWN. BUT ONLY SOME 40,000 DRAFTEES EVER SERVED IN THE MILITARY. IT WAS A VOLUNTEERS' WAR, AFTER ALL...

PRISONERS OF WAR, UNION AND CONFEDERATE, SUFFERED FROM DISEASE, HUNGER AND OVER-CROWDING. AT ANDERSONVILLE, GEORGIA, A DAY'S RATION WAS A PINT OF COARSE CORN MEAL AND A TABLESPOON OF PEAS. 13,000 PRISONERS DIED IN ONE YEAR. AFTER THE WAR, THE CAMP COMMANDER WAS EXECUTED AS A WAR CRIMINAL.

EXPOSED TO UNFAMILIAR *COLD*, THOUSANDS OF CONFEDERATE PRISONERS DIED IN NORTHERN PRISONS.

BLACK SOLDIERS CAPTURED IN THE SOUTH WERE OFTEN EXECUTED. AFTER FREDERICK DOUGLASS COMPLAINED TO LINCOLN, LINCOLN THREATENED REPRISAL AGAINST CONFEDERATE PRISONERS. BUT HE NEVER TOOK ACTION.

"...ONCE BEGUN, I DO NOT KNOW WHERE SUCH A MEASURE WOULD STOP..."

WHEN U.S. GRANT WAS APPOINTED GENERAL-IN-CHIEF OF THE UNION ARMIES, HE SENT GENERAL WILLIAM TECUMSEH SHERMAN TO SUBDUE THE REBEL STATE OF GEORGIA... SHERMAN, HERO OF THE COSTLY UNION VICTORY AT SHILOH, HAD NO RESPECT FOR MILITARY TRADITION. HE PRACTISED **TOTAL WAR** AGAINST THE CIVILIAN POPULATION, LAYING WASTE TO CROPS, LOOTING STORES AND HOUSES, DESTROYING ANYTHING OF USE TO THE CONFEDERATE ARMY.

SHERMAN'S 62,000 SOLDIERS MARCHED TO THE SEA IN A PATH OF DEVASTATION SIX MILES WIDE. THE SOUTH NEVER FORGOT.

"SHERMAN'S NECK-TIES"

FORAGERS SCOURED THE COUNTRYSIDE DAILY, LOOTING PIGS, CATTLE, CHICKENS, FLOUR, BUTTER WINE. RUNAWAY SLAVES FOLLOWED THE TROOP AND WERE FED ON THE PLUNDER.

"TO MY SMOKE-HOUSE, MY DAIRY, MY PANTRY AND CELLAR LIKE FAMISHED WOLVES THEY CAME, BREAKING LOCKS AND WHATEVER IS IN THE WAY..."

SHERMAN'S MEN BURNED BRIDGES, RIPPED UP RAILROAD TRACK AND TORE DOWN TELEGRAPH POLES ~ SMASHING CONFEDERATE TRANSPORT AND COMMUNICATIONS.

IN LATE DECEMBER 1864, SHERMAN WIRED PRESIDENT LINCOLN:

"I BEG TO PRESENT YOU AS A CHRISTMAS GIFT, THE CITY OF SAVANNAH"

SALOON - BILLIARDS

1ST BANK OF

THERE WAS UNINTENDED DESTRUCTION AS WELL~ ABANDONED STOVES AND FIREPLACES IGNITED WHOLE TOWNS. SOME STRUCTURES WERE SPARED ~ IN ATLANTA A POOL HALL WAS LEFT **INTACT** NEXT TO A DEMOLISHED BANK.

WAR IS HELL

THE CIVIL WAR WAS A TRAGIC CHAPTER IN THE HISTORY OF NATIVE AMERICANS. FORCED FROM THEIR LANDS LIKE WILD ANIMALS BY EUROPEAN COLONISTS, PUSHED TO BARREN TERRITORIES AND IMPOVERISHED BY BROKEN TREATIES, SOME TRIBES JOINED THE CONFEDERACY, ATTACKING UNION TROOPS. ORDERED TO CONTROL THE NAVAJO, IN 1864 KIT CARSON DROVE THOUSANDS ON THE DEADLY "LONG MARCH." LITTLE CROW OF THE DAKOTA LED A FAILED UPRISING. 300 OF HIS WARRIORS WERE SENTENCED TO HANGING. ABRAHAM LINCOLN PARDONED ALL BUT 39 OF THEM...

WHEN THE CIVIL WAR ENDED, TRIBAL LANDS WERE SEIZED AS WAR REPARATIONS. BY 1865, MORE THAN 10,000 INDIANS LANGUISHED IN REFUGEE CAMPS. ALL THE MAJOR TRIBES HAD SEEN THEIR LEADERSHIP AND SOURCES OF INCOME DESTROYED.

ABRAHAM LINCOLN HAD A GENEROUS HEART AND ABIDING FAITH IN THE PROMISE OF THE UNITED STATES. BUT IN HIS LIFETIME, THAT PROMISE WAS NOT EXTENDED TO THE NATIVE AMERICANS...

147

CHAPTER FIVE
LINCOLN'S LEGACY

W.E.B. Du Bois began the last paragraph of his classic history *Black Reconstruction* (1935) with these words, some of the wisest in American scholarship:

The most magnificent drama in the last thousand years of human history is the transportation of ten million human beings out of dark beauty of their mother continent into the new-found Eldorado of the West. They descended into Hell; and in the third century they arose from the dead, in the finest effort to achieve democracy of the working millions which this world had ever seen.

As DuBois suggests, a different outcome in the American South after the war—a true success for Reconstruction—would have sent a powerful message of multiracial democracy at a time when European colonialism was racing through Africa and Asia, leaving a trail of destroyed lives numbering in the millions. The colonizers were, as we now know, also planting seeds for the ecological destruction of precious rainforests and countless species of plants and animals. The costs of the American failure have remained beyond counting.

By a grotesque turn of popular misunderstanding, the greatest accomplishment of the Civil War era and the following decade was turned on its head, treating Reconstruction as the *wrongful* rise of African Americans to something like equal status and hailing the return of whites to power. This misunderstanding, reinforced by the works of many biased scholars but also by American media and especially films, from *Birth of a Nation* (1915) to *Gone With the Wind* (1939), took more than a century to overturn. In the process, the understanding of Abraham Lincoln changed and has since changed dramatically again.

Even before the end of the war, Lincoln became known to millions of people around the world as "the Great Emancipator." A counter-memory in the white South raised Robert E. Lee and Stonewall Jackson to legendary status and characterized the Confederate defeat as a glorious "lost cause." Lincoln had not, of course, willingly sought the goals of abolitionism, including interracial democracy in the South; those goals had been thrust upon him. Still, the annual outpouring of patriotic speeches on Lincoln's Birthday, still celebrated in some states, and the designation of Illinois as the "Land of Lincoln," elevated the former frontier boy nearly to the heights of adoration accorded to George Washington. Whereas the first president had established the republic, Lincoln saved it. From a later perspective, Lincoln maintained the status of national savior also achieved by Franklin Roosevelt.

ROBERT E. LEE

Did Lincoln tread on civil liberties, setting a dangerous precedent for the sweeping political repression that accompanied World War I? Did he fail to move quickly and decisively toward African-American emancipation and true citizenship, setting up the nation for enduring racism in the South, as well as segregation in jobs, voting rights, and public facilities in many parts of the nation? These criticisms are part of Lincoln's legacy to the present day, if offset by his martyrdom and personal suffering.

A grand reform coalition of free blacks, abolitionists, supporters of women's rights, and leaders of the emerging labor movement seemed, for a brief moment in the late 1860s and early 1870s, to promise a different future for the nation. Most if not all of them supporters of Lincoln, they represented the possibility of a democracy fully formed in terms of race, class, and gender. But the momentum for such wide-scale social change faded just a few years before the end of Reconstruction, leaving behind disillusionment and division. Each reform movement went its own way, to the detriment of all parts. The nation had escaped the worst dangers, but it had not been redeemed.

THE FOURTEENTH AMENDMENT

The unfinished plans for Reconstruction stood highest among the contradictions of Lincoln's legacy because they pressed so painfully upon all American life at the end of the 1860s. Lincoln had enraged many fellow Republicans with his Proclamation of Amnesty and Reconstruction in December, 1863. Considering it urgent to bring wavering Southern whites back into the fold, he offered not only pardons but the return of all property except for slaves. When vows of allegiance in any Southern state reached 10% of its 1860 vote total, according to Lincoln's proposal, the elected government of the state would be officially recognized, as long as slavery had been abolished. Radical Republicans in Congress resisted his plan, however, calling for loyalty oaths from 50% of white males in any seceding state—an unlikely level to be reached. Lincoln declined to sign this measure or to veto it outright, allowing it to die in a "pocket veto" with the end of the congressional session.

One other factor, seemingly personal, helped shape the next phases of legislative developments. Roger Taney, Chief Justice of the Supreme Court appointed by Andrew Jackson, had written the Dred Scott decision and was a confirmed believer in white supremacy. His death in October, 1864, therefore opened up the high court to a fresh breath of democracy, and Lincoln responded by nominating the most radical member of his cabinet, Salmon Chase. Shortly thereafter, Charles Sumner brought the first African-American attorney to plead a case before the Supreme Court, John Rock. His mere presence in the high court was evidence of the nation's progress.

The Fourteenth Amendment, adopted in July, 1866, might be said to capture Lincoln's best hopes for people of color, broadening the definition of citizenship specifically to include them and implying that Southern states seeking readmission to the Union would be compelled to agree to the provisions. No rights could be taken away, and the voting power of a state would be reduced by any attempt to halt African-American males from casting ballots. The Fifteenth Amendment, passed by Congress in 1869 and ratified in February, 1870, further guaranteed that the right of citizenship should not be abridged "on account of race, color or previous condition of servitude."

Lincoln's legacy of conflict with Radical Republicans was underlined—and undermined—by his successor, Andrew Johnson of Tennessee. Himself the owner of several slaves, Johnson nevertheless despised the plantation masters and remained loyal to the Union in the war. In the aftermath, however, he stood on the side of Democrats and "moderate" Republicans, seeking to build a coalition that would ensure white supremacy in the nation against all threats of equal black participation. Not only was Johnson an avowed racist, but he was narrow-minded, egotistical, and unable or unwilling to work with Congress on Reconstruction. The conflict between Congress and Johnson in the years following the war triggered the first impeachment proceedings against an American president. By a margin of only one vote in the Senate, Johnson retained his office, and Radical Republican Benjamin Wade, president pro tem of the Senate, missed the chance to become a nation-changing pro-black president.

Would a Radical Republican at the helm have changed Southern history in particular, ensuring the rights of African-Americans to exert the full influence of their legitimate voting power? Would Lincoln, had he lived, have blessed such a large-scale transfer of power after his own presidency ended? Such questions rank among the greatest imponderables in American history, and still weigh heavily on American democracy in the twenty-first century.

But make no mistake, the America of the 1870s was not the America of 1860. African-Americans held office at every level of Southern government—as long as Reconstruction lasted. They went to school, they served on juries, they owned at least some land, and in all these, they were assisted by thousands of mostly young people, idealists coming from the North. Nurses, ministers, teachers, small businesspeople—only a small number of them could be accurately described as "carpetbaggers" coming south to plunder a conquered people. The rest were visionaries risking life and limb to make a difference. Many, in fact, were African-Americans determined to help their own people.

The wonders of a democratic system that surely would have stirred Lincoln did not last. Southern whites abhorred the changes in racial status during Reconstruction, perhaps most of all the sight of armed black men in uniform. They responded with rage and violence, often under the banner of Christianity. Terror by men in white hoods— cross burnings, lynching, and castration— accompanied by wild celebrations in which sheriffs and police looked on in approval— this was the real look of what was proudly called the "New South."

The end of the war and the presidency of Ulysses S. Grant (1869-77) marked a geological shift within the Republican Party. The balance that Lincoln had sought to retain had passed. Business—mostly big business—ruled. Republicans continued to wave "the bloody flag," winning elections by labeling Democrats

PRESIDENT
ULYSSES SIMPSON GRANT

as traitors. The Grand Army of the Republic, the first veterans' group to gain national status and influence, assisted former Union soldiers in countless ways, while the war's most notorious business contractors continued to build upon their ill-gotten fortunes.

By the time James Garfield, an erstwhile Radical Republican, assumed the presidency in 1880, Republican idealism had been stripped away entirely. Serving the interests of business was his truest cause. Garfield's assassination in 1881, by contrast to Lincoln's, brought out few mourners and had little effect on American life. The next great reformer to aspire to the White House was Democrat William Jennings Bryan, who denounced entrenched interests in 1896 and again in 1900. As a faithful Democrat, however, he did not speak out for black equality or against the ghastly, ongoing parade of Southern lynchings.

The Populist movement and People's Party, embracing poor Southern whites and blacks but in separate battalions, seemed poised, at least for a few years in the 1890s, to upset the two-party system and bring real democracy into American political life. Alas, the Populists were cheated out of votes, sometimes through violence. Unable to create an independent electoral force, Populists "fused" with Republicans in parts of the South and Democrats in parts of the West, adding to the contradictions. The Populists collapsed as a political movement before the end of the century, and black political leaders stayed largely within the ranks of the Republican Party, garnering mostly patronage appointments. Lincoln's next wartime successor, Southern-raised Woodrow Wilson, had written a heroizing biography of Robert E. Lee before his White House days, declined even to meet with black leaders, and oversaw the rigid segregation of Washington, D.C.

In the longer trajectory of progressive Republicans arising from Lincoln's own Midwest, Wisconsin governor and senator Robert M. La Follette would rank highest. Curiously enough, the La Follette family had moved to Hardin County, Kentucky, around the same time as the Lincolns. In fact, the parents of the future progressive leader were actually neighbors of Lincoln's own parents. With the family's move to southern Wisconsin, a day's ride by horse from Illinois, young Bob La Follette was only six when the Civil War broke out. A poor farm boy beaten by his stepfather, the young idealist became a sterling orator during his college years (made possible by the Morrill Act, passed under Lincoln) and captivating crowds with humorous monologues and the recitation of poetry. He, too, turned to a career in law and to the Republican Party. Regarded even by his enemies as kindly, known to be an ardent supporter of the rights of women and African-Americans, La Follette arrived at a moment in history when Republicans still bested Democrats on both scores. He also worked to defend Indian tribal rights, something Lincoln had largely neglected.

La Follette's historic parting-of-the-ways with another of Lincoln's successors, Theodore Roosevelt, told much about the changes that had taken place since the 1860s. Each of the two reformers sought the 1912 nomination as a progressive, challenging the corporate-dominated politics that the two-party system had come to embrace. La Follette and his supporters had transformed Wisconsin's state government, making it more open to the public, more democratic, and more efficient in protecting the health of citizens, including factory workers. Roosevelt, rising to fame in the Spanish-American War, waged war on business trusts and hailed military action abroad, wherever Americans could spread their influence, as proof of national virility. TR also made groundbreaking contributions to American conservation, but he believed in the supremacy of empire above all. La Follette, by contrast, had concluded that empires of all kinds had become a menace to democracy and global peace. An opponent of US entry into World War I, La Follette devoted his last campaign, in 1924, to a presidential campaign on the revived Progressive Party ticket. He carried only Wisconsin and died of exhaustion within months of the election. Self-described progressive Republicans of the La Follette or Lincoln type could still be found in the Plains States, but not many after World War II. Their day had passed.

Above all, of course, it was Martin Luther King, Jr., who picked up the staff of liberty where it had fallen after the Civil War. The Reverend King, in his own scant time before assassination, had quoted Lincoln frequently and had sought, in the same strategic sense as his predecessor, to use the Declaration of Independence and the Constitution as levers to force racist society into retreat. In a deeper sense, the theological Lincoln of wartime, wrapped in the Old Testament and the judgment of a sinning nation, was not far from the King of the 1950s and 1960s. By that time, the world judged America for its claims to virtue, as a champion of human freedom, but could not overlook its less-than-virtuous racial practices. King added the dimension of New Testament redemption to the dialogue, if only white Americans could respond to the legacy of sin rather than take refuge in denial, or worse.

Often it fell to more confrontational leaders to carry on the tasks of the abolitionists. A. Philip Randolph, the founder and president of the railroad porters' union, organized a march on Washington during the war in 1942, called off only when President Franklin Roosevelt agreed to changes in the conditions of African-Americans involved in the conflict. Malcolm X, imprisoned for refusing to serve in the armed forces during the Korean War, took on a new identity as the champion of a separate black nation-to-be and turned radical reformer before his murder in 1965. The Black Panthers, pursued, persecuted, and sometimes murdered by local law enforcement officials or the FBI, made African-American demands for equality and fair treatment heard loud and clear. Through the decades, the barriers of segregation fell one by one, even as racially biased leaders kept the reins of authority in most of the South and across much of the political spectrum elsewhere, Republican to Democrat. The Civil Rights and Black Power movements of the 1960s compelled President Lyndon B. Johnson to continue in the Lincoln tradition, but also enabled him to do so.

The rest of the twentieth century, marked mainly by political retrenchment, saw Lincoln's name and his words invoked repeatedly, though often against causes he would have championed. Perhaps the final irony in political terms was that the Republicans became a white, conservative, Southern-based party with sympathies tilting—sometimes openly—to the "Lost Cause" myth of the Confederacy or the values associated with it.

In a broader context, it might be argued that the final battle in the global War Against Slavocracy was fought in 1988, far from US shores, in rural Angola. The armies of the last outright, constitutionally mandated white regime, in what was then Rhodesia, joined forces with the apartheid government of South Africa, fought together against an assortment of black African forces led in part by a Cuban brigade—and lost. In the aftermath, formal white rule and apartheid were doomed.

Lincoln's vision of a productive capitalism, outdated by the late twentieth-century transfer of industry abroad and the conversion of an industrial economy into a service-driven economy, no longer served African-American interests. Incarceration, dubbed by entertainer and activist Harry Belafonte as the "new slavery," accompanied a fresh wave of voting-rights denials in a highly polarized two-part party system. A Supreme Court decision in 2013 seemed to grant Southern states in particular the right to enact a wide array of laws limiting the participation of African-Americans (as well as the elderly, the young, the poor, and foreign-born) in the electoral process. Other states under the control of the "Party of Lincoln" followed suit. History had once more regressed, and predictably, the democratic failures of post-Civil War days returned.

The gap between the wealthy and the poor, meanwhile, expanded from the late 1970s and reached record levels, as well-paying blue collar jobs largely disappeared. Corporate executives and armies of white-collar professionals, well-educated and well-connected, grew wealthier than ever before. Millions of single black mothers bore the brunt of the new poverty, much as the wives of former slaves had carried it when their partners died or moved on in search of paying jobs. The growth of minority populations and the arrival of new immigrants promised to make non-whites a majority in the nation by the middle of the twenty-first century, a stunning shift. But it was difficult, even in an age of black celebrities in film, television, music, and sports, to see the growth of real racial equality in everyday life.

The election and reelection of Barack Obama to the presidency in 2008 and 2012 brought a sense of relief, at least briefly, to a nation weary of racial controversy and conflict. Yet suspicion and hatred, if not gross discrimination, had already turned toward Muslims, the most recent "outsiders" viewed as a threat to the social order. And the gap between rich and poor continued to expand, with no changes in sight. Was this the America upon which Abraham Lincoln had staked his devotion and his very life to save? The question hangs fire.

GETTYSBURG WAS THE TURNING POINT OF THE CIVIL WAR, THO NO ONE REALIZED IT AT THE TIME. WITH GRANT'S VICTORIES IN THE WEST AND SHERMAN PRESSING THE SOUTH, THE CONFEDERACY WAS FAILING...

VICTORY AND VENGEANCE

THE UNION NAVAL BLOCKADE KEPT SUPPLIES FROM REACHING SOUTHERN PORTS. BILLS ISSUED AS *CONFEDERATE CURRENCY* LOST VALUE. BY 1864, A BARREL OF FLOUR COST $250.00, A BAR OF SOAP $50.00...

PAMPERED PLANTATION LADIES CUT UP THEIR CARPETS TO MAKE BLANKET FOR LEE'S COLD AND HUNGRY MEN.

BUT IN THE NORTH, THERE WAS NO THRILL OF TRIUMPH. AFTER 3 YEARS, PEOPLE HAD LOST THEIR TASTE FOR WAR. THEY SCANNED THE ENDLESS LISTS OF WOUNDED AND DEAD.

WAR PROFITEERS MADE FORTUNES SELLING SOMETIMES SHODDY GOODS TO THE UNION AR BUT PRICES SOARED, AND WORKERS WAG! DID NOT KEEP PACE.

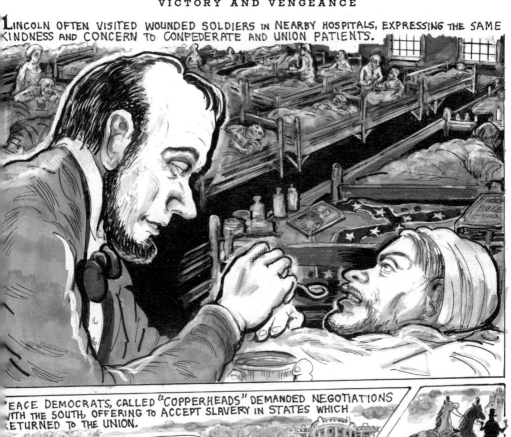

LINCOLN OFTEN VISITED WOUNDED SOLDIERS IN NEARBY HOSPITALS, EXPRESSING THE SAME KINDNESS AND CONCERN TO CONFEDERATE AND UNION PATIENTS.

PEACE DEMOCRATS, CALLED "COPPERHEADS" DEMANDED NEGOTIATIONS WITH THE SOUTH, OFFERING TO ACCEPT SLAVERY IN STATES WHICH RETURNED TO THE UNION.

THE WAR WOULD END *TOMORROW* IF WE JUST DUMPED *EMANCIPATION!*

AS THE PRESIDENTIAL ELECTION OF 1864 APPROACHED, SHERMAN WAS STALLED AT ATLANTA, AND GRANT PINNED DOWN IN THE SIEGE OF RICHMOND. ABRAHAM LINCOLN DID NOT EXPECT TO BE RE-ELECTED. HE WAS NOT EVEN CERTAIN OF THE REPUBLICAN PARTY'S *NOMINATION.*

BUT LINCOLN'S RIVALS COULD NOT SETTLE ON ONE CANDIDATE. SO HE WAS NOMINATED BY DEFAULT A 2ND TIME AND CHOSE A SOUTHERN DEMOCRAT AS HIS VICE-PRESIDENT~ ANDREW JOHNSON.

~ELECT~ Lincoln-Johnson 1864 for UNITY and PEACE

MAJOR GENERAL "LITTLE MAC" for McCLELLAN PRESIDENT

THE DEMOCRATS CHOSE GENERAL McCLELLAN—AS ARROGANT AND UNCOOPERATIVE AS EVER...

GRANT ADVANCED, SHERMAN SPLIT THE SOUTH, THE CONFEDERACY STRANGL IN DIRE STRAITS. BY ELECTION TIME, LINCOLN WAS HAILED AS A WINNER. BUT THE REPUBLICANS TOOK NO CHANCES. THEY PASSED LAWS SO UNION SOLDIERS COULD VOTE IN CAMP AND PROVIDED TRAINS FOR FURLOUGHE SOLDIERS TO RETURN HOME TO VOTE.

IN EARLY NOVEMBER 1864, LINCOLN WON HIS 2ND TERM BY A WIDE MARGIN. BUT BEFORE MAKING PEACE WITH THE SOUTH, HE WANTED TO CHISEL EMANCIPATION INTO THE U.S. CONSTITUTION. A FIRST ATTEMPT TO PASS AN AMENDMENT FAILED. NOW WITH THE WIND OF HISTORY AT HIS BACK, LINCOLN OFFERED DEALS AND TWISTED ARMS... WOMENS' RIGHTS PIONEERS SUSAN B. ANTHONY AND ELIZABETH CADY STANTON PRESENTED A PETITION WITH 400,000 SIGNATURES DEMANDING CONGRESS PUT AN END TO SLAVERY...

"NEITHER SLAVERY NOR INVOLUNTARY SERVITUDE SHALL EXIST WITHIN THE UNITED STATES..."

ON JANUARY 31, 1865, THE 13TH AMENDMENT WAS PASSED BY CONGRES OUTLAWING SLAVERY FOR ALL TIME.

CONGRESSMEN WEPT. BLACK CITIZENS CHEERED THE VOTE FROM THE PUBLIC GALLERY.

MEN THREW THEIR HATS IN THE AIR. LADIES WAVED THEIR HANDKERCHIEFS.

MARCH 4, 1865 ~ ABRAHAM LINCOLN'S 2ND INAUGURATION ~ IN HIS SPEECH, LINCOLN INVOKED OLD TESTAMENT JUSTICE TO EXPLAIN THE SUFFERING OF THE CIVIL WAR...

"WE HOPE THAT THIS MIGHTY SCOURGE OF WAR MAY SPEEDILY PASS AWAY... YET IF GOD WILLS, EVERY DROP OF BLOOD DRAWN WITH THE LASH, SHALL BE PAID BY ANOTHER DRAWN WITH THE SWORD."

"WITH MALICE TOWARD NONE, WITH CHARITY TOWARD ALL... LET US BIND UP THE NATION'S WOUNDS..."

LINCOLN LOOKED FORWARD TO A NEW ERA OF PEACE...

FREDERICK DOUGLASS WAS IN THE CROWD LISTENING TO THE SPEECH AND AFTERWARD HE HURRIED TO THE WHITE HOUSE TO CONGRATULATE LINCOLN...

AND JUST WHERE DA YA THINK YOU'RE GOING, BUDDY?!?

FREDERICK DOUGLASS IS DETAINED BY OFFICERS AT THE DOOR!!

FREDERICK DOUGLASS WAS SOON ESCORTED TO THE ELEGANT EAST ROOM.

"HOW DID YOU LIKE MY ADDRESS? THERE IS NO MAN WHOSE OPINION I VALUE MORE THAN YOURS."

★ FUN FACT: LINCOLN AND DOUGLASS, BOTH SELF-EDUCATED, STUDIED THE SAME POPULAR PUBLIC-SPEAKING MANUAL ~ CALEB BINGHAM'S 1816 THE COLUMBIAN ORATOR.

As the CONFEDERACY FLAILED in its DEATH THROES, the NATION'S CAPITAL was ABUZZ WITH THREATS and RUMOURS...MANY SLEPT UNEASILY... LINCOLN REPORTED THIS DREAM TO A FRIEND AND FORMER LAW PARTNER:

"I HAD BEEN UP WAITING for IMPORTANT DISPATCHES from the FRONT... I SOON BEGAN to DRE[AM] I HEARD SUBDUED SOBS...BUT THE MOURNERS WERE INVISIBLE... I WENT FROM ROOM to ROO[M] NO LIVING PERSON WAS IN SIGHT. I SAW LIGHT in ALL THE ROOMS. EVERY OBJECT WAS FAMILI[AR] TO ME... WHERE WERE ALL THE PEOPLE GRIEVING AS THOUGH HEARTS WOULD BREAK?

"I KEPT ON UNTIL I REACHED the EAST ROOM. BEFORE ME WAS A CATAFALQU[E] ON WHICH RESTED A CORPSE WRAPPED IN FUNERAL VESTMENTS. AROUND IT WERE STATIONED SOLDIERS ACTING AS GUARDS...THERE WAS A THRONG of PEOPLE,...GAZING MOURNFULLY UPON THE CORPSE, WHOSE FACE WAS COVERED... "

"...THEN CAME A LOUD BURST of GRIEF, WHICH WOKE ME FROM MY DREAM... "

HIS MEN STARVING, ALL ROUTES BLOCKED, ROBERT E. LEE DISPATCHED A HORSEMAN WAVING A *WHITE FLAG*.

APRIL 9, 1865 ~ APPOMATTOX COURTHOUSE, VIRGINIA

LEE WORE HIS LAST GOOD UNIFORM, GRANT A DUSTY PRIVATE'S JACKET. THE TERMS OF SURRENDER WERE SIMPLE AND GENEROUS...

> YOUR MEN MAY *KEEP* THEIR HORSES FOR SPRING PLANTING...

ONLOOKERS APPLAUDED THE UNION VICTORY. BUT GRANT HUSHED THE CELEBRATION.

> ..THE WAR IS *OVER*. THE REBELS ARE OUR COUNTRYMEN AGAIN..."

BUT NOT ALL CONFEDERATE LOYALISTS GAVE UP THE FIGHT. RAIDS CONTINUED IN THE RURAL WEST. CONSPIRATORS PLOTTED.

ROOMS TO LET

JOHN WILKES BOOTH

ONE GROUP MET AT MARY SURRATT'S BOARDINGHOUSE IN WASHINGTON, D.C., LED BY THE DASHING ACTOR JOHN WILKES BOOTH.

LESS THAN A WEEK AFTER LEE'S SURRENDER, ABRAHAM LINCOLN ANNOUNCED PLANS TO GO TO THE THEATRE, TO SEE THE *HIT* COMEDY <u>OUR AMERICAN COUSIN</u>.

APRIL 14, 1865 ~ FORD'S THEATRE

JOHN WILKES BOOTH HID IN AN UPSTAIRS BACK CORRIDOR...

AN EVENING OUT WATCHING A PLAY WAS A RARE TREAT FOR MARY.

LINCOLN'S GUARD TOOK A BREAK DOWNSTAIRS. AS THE AUDIENCE ROARED WITH LAUGHTER, BOOTH ENTERED THE PRESIDENTIAL BOX AND FIRED HIS PISTOL POINT-BLANK

THUS ALWAYS TO *TYRANTS!*

BOOTH LEAPED DOWN TO THE STAGE, BREAKING HIS LEG.

SOLDIERS CARRIED LINCOLN ACROSS THE STREET TO THE PETERSEN HOUSE, WHERE HIS TALL BODY HAD TO BE STRETCHED *DIAGONALLY* ACROSS A LODGER'S BED. PHYSICIANS STRUGGLED TO SAVE THE FALLEN PRESIDENT...

THE WOUND IS *MORTAL*. HE CANNOT RECOVER...

BOOTH ESCAPED ON A HORSE WAITING IN THE ALLEY. A WEEK LATER HE WAS TRAPPED IN A BURNING BARN IN VIRGINIA AND SHOT TO DEATH BY UNION TROOPS.

MEANWHILE THE NATION MOURNED. BELLS TOLLED, FLAGS WERE LOWERED TO HALF-MAST, SOLDIERS FIRED A 21 GUN SALUTE. ABRAHAM LINCOLN'S BODY WAS CARRIED TO THE CAPITAL BUILDING, WHERE HE LAY IN STATE FOR THREE DAYS.

WAIL!! WOE!!

APRIL 21 ~ MAY 4, 1865 A SEVEN CAR FUNERAL TRAIN LEFT WASHINGTON, TRANSPORTING ABE LINCOLN HOME TO SPRINGFIELD ILLINOIS. AS THE TRAIN NEARED, THRONGS OF MOURNERS LIT BONFIRES ALONG THE TRACKS. THE COFFIN OF LINCOLN'S BELOVED SON WILLIE, DEAD OF TYPHOID IN 1862, TRAVELED WITH HIS FATHER TO BE BURIED BESIDE HIM IN OAKRIDGE CEMETERY.

"...THOUGH DEEP, HE WAS TRANSPARENT, THOUGH STRONG, HE WAS GENTLE. HE WAS TOLERANT TOWARD THOSE WHO DIFFERED FROM HIM AND PATIENT UNDER REPROACHES... HIS GREAT MISSION WAS TO ACCOMPLISH TWO THINGS: FIRST, TO SAVE HIS COUNTRY FROM DISMEMBERMENT AND RUIN, AND, SECOND, TO FREE HIS COUNTRY FROM THE GREAT CRIME OF SLAVERY... TAKING HIM FOR ALL IN ALL, MEASURING THE TREMENDOUS MAGNITUDE OF THE WORK BEFORE HIM, INFINITE WISDOM HAS SELDOM SENT ANY MAN INTO THE WORLD BETTER SUITED FOR HIS MISSION THAN ABRAHAM LINCOLN"

~ FREDERICK DOUGLASS 1876

SHARON RUDAHL, FEBRUARY 2014

FURTHER READING

More than 15,000 books have been published about Abraham Lincoln, as well as innumerable essays, historical documents (many available on the web), and other texts. Here are a few books that are especially interesting and cogent.

DOCUMENTARY SOURCES

The Abraham Lincoln Companion. Edited by Helene Henderson, with a Foreword by Douglas L. Wilson of the Lincoln Studies Center, Knox College, Galesburg, Illinois. Detroit: Omnigraphics, 2008.

An Autobiography of Abraham Lincoln: Consisting of the Personal Portions of his Letters, Speeches and Conversations. Compiled and annotated by Nathaniel Wright Stephenson. Indianapolis: Bobbs Merrill, 1926.

Abraham Lincoln, Speeches and Writings, two volumes. New York: The Library of America, 1989.

SCHOLARLY STUDIES

Robert Bray, *Reading With Lincoln*. Carbondale: Southern Illinois University Press, 2010.

Michael Burkheimer, *Lincoln's Christianity*. Yardley, PA: Westholme Publishing, 2007.

Orville Vernon Burton, *The Age of Lincoln*. New York: Hill and Wang, 2007.

Jim Cullen, *The Civil War in Popular Culture: A Reusable Past*. Washington, D.C.: Smithsonian Press, 1995.

W.E.B. DuBois, *Black Reconstruction in America*. New York: S.A. Russell, 1935,

Eric Foner, *The Fiery Trial: Abraham Lincoln and American Slavery*. New York: W.W. Norrton, 2010.

Guy C. Fraker, *Lincoln's Ladder to the Presidency: the Eighth Judicial Circuit*. Carbondale: Southern Illinois University Press, 2010.

George McGovern, *Abraham Lincoln*. New York: Times Books, 2009.

Carl Sandburg, *Abraham Lincoln: The Prairie Years*, two volumes, New York: Harcourt, Brace and Company, 1926.

Carl Sandburg, *Abraham Lincoln: The War Years*, two volumes New York: Harcourt, Brace and Company, 1939.

THE FOR BEGINNERS® SERIES

AFRICAN HISTORY FOR BEGINNERS	ISBN 978-1-934389-18-8
ANARCHISM FOR BEGINNERS	ISBN 978-1-934389-32-4
ARABS & ISRAEL FOR BEGINNERS	ISBN 978-1-934389-16-4
ART THEORY FOR BEGINNERS	ISBN 978-1-934389-47-8
ASTRONOMY FOR BEGINNERS	ISBN 978-1-934389-25-6
AYN RAND FOR BEGINNERS	ISBN 978-1-934389-37-9
BARACK OBAMA FOR BEGINNERS, AN ESSENTIAL GUIDE	ISBN 978-1-934389-44-7
BEN FRANKLIN FOR BEGINNERS	ISBN 978-1-934389-48-5
BLACK HISTORY FOR BEGINNERS	ISBN 978-1-934389-19-5
THE BLACK HOLOCAUST FOR BEGINNERS	ISBN 978-1-934389-03-4
BLACK WOMEN FOR BEGINNERS	ISBN 978-1-934389-20-1
CHOMSKY FOR BEGINNERS	ISBN 978-1-934389-17-1
DADA & SURREALISM FOR BEGINNERS	ISBN 978-1-934389-00-3
DANTE FOR BEGINNERS	ISBN 978-1-934389-67-6
DECONSTRUCTION FOR BEGINNERS	ISBN 978-1-934389-26-3
DEMOCRACY FOR BEGINNERS	ISBN 978-1-934389-36-2
DERRIDA FOR BEGINNERS	ISBN 978-1-934389-11-9
EASTERN PHILOSOPHY FOR BEGINNERS	ISBN 978-1-934389-07-2
EXISTENTIALISM FOR BEGINNERS	ISBN 978-1-934389-21-8
FANON FOR BEGINNERS	ISBN 978-1-934389-87-4
FDR AND THE NEW DEAL FOR BEGINNERS	ISBN 978-1-934389-50-8
FOUCAULT FOR BEGINNERS	ISBN 978-1-934389-12-6
FRENCH REVOLUTIONS FOR BEGINNERS	ISBN 978-1-934389-91-1
GENDER & SEXUALITY FOR BEGINNERS	ISBN 978-1-934389-69-0
GLOBAL WARMING FOR BEGINNERS	ISBN 978-1-934389-27-0
GREEK MYTHOLOGY FOR BEGINNERS	ISBN 978-1-934389-83-6
HEIDEGGER FOR BEGINNERS	ISBN 978-1-934389-13-3
THE HISTORY OF CLASSICAL MUSIC FOR BEGINNERS	ISBN 978-1-939994-26-4
THE HISTORY OF OPERA FOR BEGINNERS	ISBN 978-1-934389-79-9
ISLAM FOR BEGINNERS	ISBN 978-1-934389-01-0
JANE AUSTEN FOR BEGINNERS	ISBN 978-1-934389-61-4
JUNG FOR BEGINNERS	ISBN 978-1-934389-76-8
KIERKEGAARD FOR BEGINNERS	ISBN 978-1-934389-14-0
LACAN FOR BEGINNERS	ISBN 978-1-934389-39-3
LINGUISTICS FOR BEGINNERS	ISBN 978-1-934389-28-7
MALCOLM X FOR BEGINNERS	ISBN 978-1-934389-04-1
MARX'S DAS KAPITAL FOR BEGINNERS	ISBN 978-1-934389-59-1
MCLUHAN FOR BEGINNERS	ISBN 978-1-934389-75-1
NIETZSCHE FOR BEGINNERS	ISBN 978-1-934389-05-8
PAUL ROBESON FOR BEGINNERS	ISBN 978-1-934389-81-2
PHILOSOPHY FOR BEGINNERS	ISBN 978-1-934389-02-7
PLATO FOR BEGINNERS	ISBN 978-1-934389-08-9
POETRY FOR BEGINNERS	ISBN 978-1-934389-46-1
POSTMODERNISM FOR BEGINNERS	ISBN 978-1-934389-09-6
RELATIVITY & QUANTUM PHYSICS FOR BEGINNERS	ISBN 978-1-934389-42-3
SARTRE FOR BEGINNERS	ISBN 978-1-934389-15-7
SHAKESPEARE FOR BEGINNERS	ISBN 978-1-934389-29-4
STRUCTURALISM & POSTSTRUCTURALISM FOR BEGINNERS	ISBN 978-1-934389-10-2
WOMEN'S HISTORY FOR BEGINNERS	ISBN 978-1-934389-60-7
UNIONS FOR BEGINNERS	ISBN 978-1-934389-77-5
U.S. CONSTITUTION FOR BEGINNERS	ISBN 978-1-934389-62-1
ZEN FOR BEGINNERS	ISBN 978-1-934389-06-5
ZINN FOR BEGINNERS	ISBN 978-1-934389-40-9

WWW.FORBEGINNERSBOOKS.COM